MW01050960

JON BONNELL'S

# WATERS

*Leslie (140.6)*

*All my best,*

WATERSTEXAS.COM

JON BONNELL'S

# WATERS

FINE COASTAL CUISINE

JON BONNELL

PHOTOGRAPHS BY JODY HORTON

**GIBBS SMITH**
TO ENRICH AND INSPIRE HUMANKIND

TO MY DAD, WHO ALWAYS TOOK
THE TIME TO TAKE ME FISHING

First Edition
18 17 16 15 14          5 4 3 2 1

Text © 2014 Jon Bonnell
Photographs © 2014 Jody Horton

Published by
Gibbs Smith
P.O. Box 667
Layton, Utah 84041

1.800.835.4993 orders
www.gibbs-smith.com

Designed by Sheryl Dickert
Pages produced by Renee Bond
Printed and bound in China

Gibbs Smith books are printed on either recycled,
100% post-consumer waste, FSC-certified papers or
on paper produced from sustainable PEFC-certified
forest/controlled wood source. Learn more at
www.pefc.org.

Library of Congress Cataloging-in-Publication Data

Bonnell, Jon.
 Jon Bonnell's waters : fine coastal cuisine /
Jon Bonnell ; photographs by Jody Horton. — First
edition.
    pages cm
 Includes index.
 ISBN 978-1-4236-3306-8
 1. Cooking (Seafood)—Texas—Gulf Coast. I. Title.
 TX747.B2993 2014
 641.6'9097641—dc23
                              2013027904

# CONTENTS

# INTRODUCTION

Fishing has been one of my greatest passions ever since I was a kid, and the allure of the sea is impossible for me to resist. I learned how to clean a trout by age six and have been catching, cleaning and cooking seafood ever since. Whether standing knee-deep in a tumbling mountain stream in search of trout, pulling a top-water plug across the surface of a bass pond or scanning the endless horizon from a flats boat for migrating tarpon, I'm constantly either planning the next fishing trip in my head or telling stories from my last one. The waters of the world will always be my playground.

As a chef, I have a true passion for seafood, not only because of my love for the sport of fishing, but because there is always variety. When I order meat, I call the same guys and can buy the same steaks pretty much every day. When I talk to my fish suppliers however, every day is an adventure with a myriad of stories. I love to hear which captain is catching what and where—all the while wishing I could be the one pulling in the lines.

While I use some fish from sustainable aquafarms, I also love the daily challenge of finding out what's fresh and wild. I never ask my suppliers what they have in inventory. Instead, I want to know what's coming in on the boat that might make it to the dock before the FedEx cutoff time. There is simply no substitute for freshness in seafood, so the pursuit of the finest wild fish never ends for a chef.

The diversity that seafood brings to a chef is unmatched in any other category of proteins. Just when I think I've cooked it all, a new fish catches my attention and I can hardly wait to create a new dish. Usually, once I'm tired of seeing any specific fish the season tends to run out and it won't be available until the next year anyway. That's the beauty of the fish game—always changing, always a challenge, never a dull moment.

Through all of my years in teaching cooking, I've found that almost everyone I come across is afraid to cook fish for one reason or another. The seafood display in most grocery stores somehow intimidates customers in a way that the meat display does not. People can fire up the grill and pull off a decent steak with their eyes closed, but hand them a snapper, and some primitive fear wells up inside them at the thought of trying to fillet it, much less cook it. This book will ease the intimidation of working with seafood. The recipes—from simple to complex—are some of my favorites. From the many waters of the world, here's how I like to enjoy the bounty and diversity of fantastic, flippin'-fresh seafood.

## WILD, SEASONAL, SUSTAINABLE

I'm a sport-fisherman, a chef, multiple-restaurant owner, outdoorsman and conservationist, so this subject is close to my heart. In all of my dealings with fishermen, various seafood purveyors and suppliers across the country, my mission has always been the same: find the highest quality and freshest seafood for my customers while doing my best to support American fishermen and protect wild fisheries.

Without an effort by the general public, the seafood industry could quickly get out of control. Every year, someone in this country goes to jail for fishing and selling out of season; someone changes the name of a fish for a quick buck; some restaurateur serves fish that he/she knows to be in serious population decline. I'm not the type for massive regulations or red tape of any kind, but the regulations in the seafood industry are set for a reason. The federal government and individual state governments set quotas, seasons and limits to keep the public safe and the wild fish populations healthy for generations to come.

The best seafood comes from the cleanest and best-maintained waters of the world. I strongly discourage buying seafood items from inexpensive foreign aquafarms when possible, as most of them have found a way to provide the cheapest product possible with no regard for quality, health benefits or environmental impact. Some domestic aquafarming practices are fantastic (like Texas redfish and hybrid striped bass operations), but in general, I tend to avoid fish from foreign countries with too-good-to-be-true prices. I'm sure you can guess many of the likely culprits.

Since the seafood game changes with every boat that leaves the dock, it is very difficult to keep an eye on what is happening in the overall market. For anyone wishing to find out the global status of a particular fish population, I've found a resource that makes this process quite simple. As a professional, I talk to purveyors, fishermen and suppliers on a daily basis, as well as keep up with the industry news from several sources. For the consumer, the website seafoodwatch.org (also a great app for smartphones) is the best resource that I have found. Seafood Watch is kept up to date by the Monterey Bay Aquarium and makes it easy to see which fish is on the sustainable side when you have a choice in what to cook. Know your source, support American fishermen first, celebrate what the waters of the world have to offer and save plenty for the next generation. That's why I choose wild, seasonal and sustainable seafood every chance I get.

## Chef's Favorites

Throughout the book, many of my recipes call for hot sauce and pre-blended spices. I gravitate towards several favorite brands that give distinctive flavors and complexity to my dishes.

For **hot sauce,** Crystal is my favorite because it has just the right balance of acidity, heat and salt. While some hot sauce brands lend just heat, Crystal is mild and flavorful enough to use plenty without overpowering a dish. I recommend that you give Crystal a try, but if you have a brand that suits you better, feel free to substitute it in any recipes listed here.

**Texas Red Dirt Rubs** and **Waters Bay Blend** are my own brands of dry spice mixes.

The Red Dirt line includes a **Southwestern Blend,** a **Barbecue Blend** and a **Creole Blend.** You can purchase any of the Red Dirt Rubs at bonnellstexas.com, or I'm happy to share the recipe for any of these blends as well. Simply send an email to bonnellstexas.com and I'll return the recipe in Word format. There are many different spice mixes on the market that can be substituted in a pinch, but most are very heavy on the salt and none will produce the same great results we have produced at my restaurants and adapted specifically for these recipes.

There are also many different brands of **chile powder** on the market, but my go-to brand is always Pendery's because they use the best-quality chiles, no fillers and have such a great variety to choose from. I normally use their Bull Canyon blend, but El Rey, Fort Worth Blend and New Mexico Red are all great blends as well. Pendery's also adds a heat indicator on each blend to let you know the level of spice to expect, which I really like.

For spicy prepared **mustard,** I'm a Zatarain's guy. I love their intense Creole Mustard, which has quite a tangy horseradish kick. For more traditional mustards and mustard powder, I use Coleman's.

Occasionally, a good **bourbon** rounds out a sauce, and for this, I buy local Texas bourbon. I've been using TX whiskey from Firestone and Robertson and Garrison Brothers Bourbon more than anything else these days, and have a hard time just adding it to the sauce, if you know what I mean.

A word about **grits**: stone-ground are just better, and Homestead Gristmill Grits is the brand I like. Stone ground grits have more real corn flavor than anything instant. They might take longer to cook, but the trade-off in quality and flavor is well worth the effort.

## WATERS BAY BLEND  *Makes 1 3/4 cups*

*I mix this up in a big batch to keep handy.*

| | | | |
|---|---|---|---|
| 1 | teaspoon black peppercorns | 4 | tablespoons granulated garlic |
| 1 | teaspoon pink peppercorns | 1 | tablespoon onion powder |
| 1 | teaspoon white peppercorns | 1/2 | tablespoon cayenne pepper |
| 2 | teaspoons coriander seeds | 1/2 | teaspoon chili de arbol powder |
| 1 | teaspoon celery seed | 2 1/2 | tablespoons paprika |
| 10 | tablespoons sea salt | 1 | teaspoon mustard powder |
| 1 | bay leaf | 1/2 | teaspoon citric acid |
| 4 | tablespoons dill | | Pinch of ground cloves |
| 2 | tablespoons basil | | Pinch of ground nutmeg |
| 2 | tablespoons chives | | Pinch of ground ginger |
| 1 | tablespoon tarragon | | Pinch of ground allspice |

Toast the peppercorns, coriander, and celery seeds together then let cool.

Combine the toasted seeds, sea salt, bay leaf, dill, basil, chives, and tarragon in a spice mill and grind until a smooth powder is formed. Mix with all other ingredients and whisk together well. Store in an airtight container.

# CHILLED AND RAW

For the true purist, the finest way to enjoy seafood is in its raw form. Oysters or clams pulled straight from the briny sea are a culinary treat to many, needing very little enhancement or seasoning. Thinly sliced fish in the form of a crudo (dressed with oil, salt and citrus or vinegar) or carpaccio (served with a sauce) can be equally as enthralling for the seafood aficionado. Citrus-marinated raw preparations such as ceviche (marinated) or tartare (seasoned) can also be respectful of the original flavor of great seafood.

Not all seafood eaten cold has to be raw, however. In fact, ceviche, though not cooked through the application of heat, is somewhat cooked through chemistry as the acidic nature of citrus fruit "cooks" the fish. Cooked, then chilled piles of boiled shrimp, crab and lobster have been popular for years. The enticing cold seafood display nestled atop crushed ice has long been a favorite among seafood lovers and restaurateurs.

The real key to outstanding raw or chilled seafood begins, like any other seafood preparation, with superior freshness and proper handling. Shellfish, especially, have to be extremely fresh or it's not even worth talking about. Lobsters, crabs and crawfish are best steamed or boiled live, while shrimp are most commonly cleaned and frozen on the boats that catch them even before they reach shore. The most important rule for seafood: freshness is mandatory.

# CEVICHE OF GRILLED STRIPED BASS  *Serves 2*

*I love using striped bass from Texas for this dish because it is farm-raised, extremely consistent in price and quality and has a very mild flavor that takes on acidic overtones and spices very well. The texture is also perfect for an authentic ceviche. Wild striped bass (or hybrid striped bass) will also work as a substitute, as will snapper, grouper or drum. I've even used catfish in a pinch. I love getting just a bit of rustic flavor from grilling the outside of the fish briefly while leaving the inside raw.*

*The serrano is my favorite chile for this particular dish, but jalapeño or habanero peppers can be substituted; be careful to check the heat level before serving to guests or kids.*

*This dish takes 2 days to prepare, so be sure to plan ahead.*

6 ounces fresh Texas farm-raised striped bass

¼ cup finely chopped purple onion

Juice of 6 limes, divided

1 Roma tomato, seeds removed, finely diced

1 serrano chile, finely diced, seeds and veins optional*

8–10 sprigs fresh cilantro, roughly chopped

¼ teaspoon garlic powder

Pinch of salt

Pinch of freshly ground black pepper

Freshly fried corn tortilla chips sprinkled with sea salt as an accompaniment

Clean the bass well of any blood lines or skin and grill very quickly over high heat just enough to create grill marks but leaving the center completely raw. After the bass has cooled, cut into medium dice. Combine with the chopped onion and juice from 5 limes, and marinate in the refrigerator overnight. On the second day, drain the juice and discard. Then add remaining ingredients, including the juice of the remaining lime. Serve chilled, with tortilla chips.

*\*Leaving the seeds and veins in the serrano will give a great level of spice, but all or some may be removed to make this dish milder if desired.*

# OYSTERS ON THE HALF SHELL WITH SOUTHWESTERN SERRANO SAUCE  *Serves 2–4*

*I love to serve oysters on the half shell, especially at parties. Opening oysters right before eating them seems like the truest expression of the sea and provides a little taste of the ocean in every bite. The sauce possibilities are endless, really, but these are a few of my favorites. If I had to pick just one, it would be the southwestern serrano; it really adds the right balance of citrus acidity with a little texture and enough flavor and heat to complement the oysters, not overpower them.*

2   dozen fresh oysters

Shuck each oyster and serve on a bed of crushed ice with one of the sauces below

## SOUTHWESTERN SERRANO SAUCE  *Makes $3/4$ cup*

Juice of 3 lemons

Juice of 2 limes

2   serrano peppers, seeds optional, minced

1   small Roma tomato, seeds removed, finely diced

1   small shallot, minced

$3/4$   teaspoon Texas Red Dirt Rub, Southwestern Blend (see page 9)

$1/2$   teaspoon salt

Combine all ingredients in a mixing bowl and allow to marinate for 25–30 minutes.

## CHAMPAGNE MIGNONETTE  *Makes 1 cup*

2   teaspoons freshly ground black pepper

1   cup champagne vinegar

2   tablespoons minced shallots

Pinch of salt

Combine all ingredients in a mixing bowl and allow to marinate for 25–30 minutes.

## CHIPOTLE COCKTAIL SAUCE  *Makes about $1 1/4$ cups*

1   cup ketchup

$1 1/2$   teaspoons prepared horseradish

2–3   heavy shakes Worcestershire sauce

Juice of 1 lemon

1   teaspoon Dijon mustard

1   chipotle pepper (from can of chipotles in adobo sauce)

Pinch of smoked hot paprika

Combine all ingredients and puree in a blender or food processor until smooth. Strain and serve.

# WHITE GAZPACHO WITH LUMP CRAB  *Serves 6–8*

*Gazpacho and other chilled soups are some of the great treasures of summer. I love the way this creamy yet acidic soup perfectly complements the sweet and rich flavors of crabmeat. The key to making the perfect gazpacho is to use a grinder for the right consistency. Fresh vegetables can all be sent right through the grinder together to get a smooth consistency with the perfect crunch. Adding a few drops of white truffle oil (or even a touch of caviar) is a fun way to surprise dinner guests with a little extra indulgence for special occasions, but certainly is not required for this dish to be a success.*

## FOR THE SOUP:

- 2 ounces sliced almonds
- 3 large yellow tomatoes
- 2 yellow bell peppers, seeded
- 2 large cucumbers, peeled and seeded
- ½ small sweet onion
- 6 ribs celery (the lighter in color the better, no leaves)

- 1 ⅔ cups half-and-half
- 4 tablespoons extra virgin olive oil
- Juice of 4 limes
- 1 ¼ teaspoons salt
- ½ teaspoon white pepper
- ½ teaspoon white truffle oil, optional

## FOR THE GARNISH:

- 8 ounces lump crabmeat
- Juice of 1 lemon
- 1 ½ teaspoons extra virgin olive oil
- Pinch of salt

- Pinch of freshly ground black pepper
- Chopped fresh chives or chive blossoms
- Caviar, optional

Toast the almonds in a 350-degree oven for a few minutes until lightly golden brown. Pulse the toasted almonds a few times in a spice grinder or food processor until they are well chopped, almost a powder.

Run the tomatoes, peppers, cucumbers, onion, and celery through a grinder with the small plate attached. Combine with the liquid ingredients and almonds; season and whisk thoroughly to combine. Refrigerate for at least 1 hour.

Meanwhile, pick through the crab for shell pieces, then season with lemon juice, olive oil and a pinch of salt and pepper. Serve in a soup cup, mug or chilled martini glass with a sprinkle of chives or chive blossoms on top. Blue crab claws also make a great garnish for this dish, giving a little more color and adding another aspect of the crab. Let's face it, can anyone ever have too much crab?

*Note: For the ultimate indulgence, add a small amount of fine caviar to the top.*

# SCALLOP CARPACCIO WITH CITRUS AIOLI  *Serves 4*

*Scallops are extremely lean and lend themselves well to raw dishes like carpaccio and tartare. I love the little crunch that the radishes add to this dish, and the lightly flavored citrus aioli doesn't overpower the scallops. This dish is easy to make the day ahead for a dinner party: layer the plates and cover them tightly with plastic wrap. Just before serving, finish with the sauce and garnish.*

| | |
|---|---|
| 10 large fresh diver scallops | Sea salt |
| Coriander seeds | Fresh chives, snipped for garnish |
| Pink peppercorns | 1 radish, julienned, for garnish |

Clean the scallops well, being sure to remove any grit and the side muscle that can sometimes be attached. Rinse well under cold water, then pat dry with paper towels. Using a very sharp knife, slice the scallops into very thin rounds and arrange on a plate slightly overlapping in concentric circles until the plate is mostly covered. Place equal parts coriander seeds and pink peppercorns in a pepper mill together and crack the mixture (large grinds) evenly over the plate to lightly dust the scallops. Sprinkle a light coating of sea salt over the plate as well, then drizzle decoratively with the citrus aioli. Garnish with freshly snipped chives and julienned radish.

## CITRUS AIOLI  *Makes 1 1/2 cups*

| | |
|---|---|
| 3 egg yolks | Juice of 1 lime |
| 1 clove garlic | Juice of 1/2 orange |
| 1 1/2 teaspoons Dijon mustard | 1/2 teaspoon salt |
| Juice of 2 lemons | 1 cup canola oil |

Combine all ingredients, except the oil, in a blender and puree until smooth. Slowly drizzle in the oil until the mixture becomes smooth and creamy. Place inside a squirt bottle to decorate the final plate.

# HIMACHI CRUDO WITH CITRUS VINAIGRETTE    *Serves 4*

*A crudo is one of the very best ways to enjoy really fresh, sushi-quality fish. Himachi, also called yellowtail jack, has a richly flavored flesh and works exceptionally well for this type of presentation. It should go without saying that only the freshest fish can be used for this type of dish, but when it's perfectly fresh, it's the ideal way to celebrate the purest form of this great fish. Opah, tuna or salmon can be good substitutes as long as they are sushi/sashimi quality.*

6   ounces fresh sashimi-grade himachi (yellowtail jack)

Freshly ground black pepper

2   jalapeño peppers, seeds removed

½   red bell pepper

2   radishes

Pinch of salt

Carefully remove the skin and any visible blood line from the himachi and slice into very thin slivers. Fan out the slices across a chilled dinner plate and season lightly with pepper.

Cut the peppers and radishes into fine julienne strips and toss together with a pinch of salt, then dress lightly with the vinaigrette and arrange over himachi. Drizzle some of the vinaigrette over the fish and around the plate.

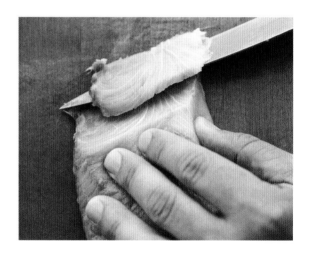

## CITRUS VINAIGRETTE    *Makes ¼ cup*

2   teaspoons lemon juice

1   teaspoon lime juice

1   teaspoon Dijon mustard

2 ½   tablespoons extra virgin olive oil

½   teaspoon Texas Red Dirt Rub, Southwestern Blend (see page 9)

Whisk all ingredients together until combined.

# STONE CRAB WITH MUSTARD SAUCE    *Serves 4–6*

*Stone crab is one of the purest of all seafoods for sheer indulgence. The Florida stone crab season opens on October 15th (my birthday), and my father and I always pick a day to celebrate by sitting down to an enormous pile of chilled claws, mustard sauce and Sauvignon Blanc. It's probably the sweetest-flavored of all crab, and I usually only eat it in its simplest form, rarely adding any more complexity. There are many different versions of the "mustard sauce" that is typically served with stone crab, but this one is my all-time favorites.*

*Florida stone crabs are unique in that they are somewhat of a catch-and-release animal. The crabs are trapped, one claw is harvested, then the crabs are tossed back into the water alive. With one claw left, they can still defend themselves and will regenerate the harvested claw, hopefully in time for the next season. If I ever develop a severe shellfish allergy, my plan is to consume my body weight in stone crab claws and die happy right on the spot.*

  2   pounds stone crab claws

Crack the claws by hitting briskly with the back side of a heavy spoon, then carefully remove some of the thick shell pieces. Serve the pre-cracked claws chilled, with plenty of mustard sauce for dipping.

## MUSTARD SAUCE    *Makes 4 cups*

| | | | | |
|---|---|---|---|---|
| 2 | cups sour cream | | 1 | tablespoon hot sauce |
| 2 | cups mayonnaise | | ¼ | teaspoon smoked sweet paprika |
| 4 | tablespoons chopped chives | | ¼ | teaspoon hot sweet paprika |
| 2 | tablespoons chopped dill | | 1½ | teaspoons Worcestershire sauce |
| 1½ | tablespoons Coleman's mustard powder | | | Juice of 1½ lemons |
| | | | ½ | tablespoon salt |

Combine all ingredients in a mixing bowl and whisk together well. Allow to sit for at least 5 minutes before serving.

# SPICY TUNA TARTARE   *Serves 4*

*The key to a great tuna tartare is the right balance of acidity, salt and spice. Although the heat level can be changed, I prefer a little spice to liven up this dish. Ahi tuna, also called yellowfin, is my preference for this dish, but bigeye tuna or even fresh albacore can be outstanding as well. The technique is simple, and can earn you big presentation points from dinner guests if you can pull off this easy ring mold preparation.*

| | | | | |
|---|---|---|---|---|
| 2 | ounces radishes, peeled and finely diced | | 1 | tablespoon Dijon mustard |
| 2 | ounces cucumber, peeled, seeded and finely diced | | 1/2 | teaspoon cayenne pepper |
| 1 | tablespoon capers, chopped | | 2 | dashes hot sauce |
| 1 | Roma tomato, seeded and finely diced | | 1/2 | teaspoon salt |
| 1 | shallot, finely diced | | 1/2 | teaspoon freshly ground black pepper |
| | Juice of 1 1/2 limes | | 8 | ounces sashimi-grade Ahi tuna, medium dice |

### FOR THE MOLD PREPARATION:

| | | | | |
|---|---|---|---|---|
| 1 | ripe avocado, diced | | 3 | tablespoons sour cream |
| | Pinch of salt | | | Freshly ground black pepper |
| | Juice of 1 lime | | 1 | ounce caviar, optional |

For the tuna, combine all ingredients, except for the tuna, in a bowl and mix well. Just before serving, combine this mixture with the tuna and serve quickly or the tuna will "cook" too much and change in appearance and texture.

Season the avocado with a pinch of salt and a light squeeze of lime, then place one layer in the center of a plate inside a ring mold. Season the sour cream with a squeeze of lime juice and a pinch of salt and pepper as well.

Scoop a couple ounces of the tuna mixture to form the next layer in the ring mold and gently press down with the back of a spoon to smooth out the mixture. Gently remove the ring mold, then top with a dollop of the sour cream mixture and, optionally, a few eggs of caviar.

# TARTARE TRIO, SALMON, SCALLOP AND OPAH   *Serves 6–8*

*Any of these tartare preparations can work well alone, but I prefer to serve all three on a platter together as a little sampler of chilled seafood. Each one has a different flavor, making the overall spread a more complex and fun way to enjoy a light snack. It's a perfect way to start a light lunch, served in the middle of the table for everyone to sample. A light and crisp white wine like Sauvignon Blanc pairs perfectly with this dish.*

## FOR THE SCALLOPS:

½ pound fresh scallops, rinsed and patted dry with paper towel

1 teaspoon sesame oil

Pinch of cayenne pepper

1 teaspoon lemon zest

Juice of 1 lemon

1 teaspoon soy sauce

2 tablespoons mayonnaise

1 tablespoon chopped chives

1 teaspoon toasted sesame seeds

Dice the scallops into small cubes and combine with all ingredients. Allow to marinate in the fridge for 30–40 minutes before serving.

## FOR THE SALMON:

½ pound fresh salmon, cleaned, rinsed and patted dry with a paper towel

2 tablespoons chopped fresh dill

1 small shallot, minced

Juice of 2 lemons

2 tablespoons capers, drained and chopped

Pinch of sea salt

Dice the salmon into small cubes and combine with all ingredients. Allow to marinate in the fridge for 30–40 minutes before serving.

## FOR THE OPAH:

½ pound opah fillet, cleaned, rinsed and patted dry with a paper towel

1 tablespoon extra virgin olive oil

Juice and zest of 2 limes

2 teaspoons soy sauce

1 tablespoon hot sauce

1 jalapeño pepper, seeded and diced

3 green onions, white and green parts finely diced

3–4 sprigs fresh cilantro, roughly chopped

Dice the opah into small cubes and combine with all ingredients. Allow to marinate in the fridge for 30–40 minutes before serving.

# SMOKED TROUT PÂTÉ   *Serves 6–8*

*The stovetop smoker is a great tool for this dish. It's the perfect size to fit 1 to 2 trout fillets and requires very little setup—and more importantly, cleanup! And for roughly $35, it's an inexpensive way to add rich smoke flavor to many foods without the hassle of firing up the big outdoor pit. I like to serve this dish at casual gatherings as a light but flavorful spread for crackers or bread. It pairs really well with oaky California Chardonnay.*

| | | | |
|---|---|---|---|
| 1 | 8-ounce rainbow trout fillet | 2 | tablespoons chopped fresh dill |
| 5 | ounces cream cheese | | Juice of 1 lemon |
| 2 | ounces heavy cream | ½ | teaspoon chipotle powder |
| 1 | small shallot, diced | 1 | teaspoon Waters Bay Blend (see page 10) |

Be sure the trout fillet is cleaned well of all bones. Place fillet in a smoker and cook for 15 minutes over pecan wood chips. Once the fish is smoked, allow to cool, then flake the meat carefully off of the skin. Combine all remaining ingredients in a food processor and pulse until the mixture is smooth. Add the smoked trout and pulse just until combined. Serve with your favorite crackers or flatbreads and a small spreading knife.

# Octopus Carpaccio with Southwestern Mustard Vinaigrette   *Serves 6–8*

*I first tried octopus while on vacation in Argentina, mainly because I'd never seen anything like it. It made such an impression on me that I had to create my own version. Octopus may seem strange to many people, but its meat is very tasty and easy to like if properly cooked. Unlike most carpaccio dishes, this one does not use raw meat. The octopus must be cooked first and then frozen in a log shape before being sliced very thinly on a deli slicer. The result is the full flavor of octopus, with a very tender texture. I love to pair this flavor with a tart, spicy and salty vinaigrette to make the dish a little more well-rounded.*

*While you can actually buy logs of frozen cooked octopus ready to slice from companies like seafoods.com, cooking it yourself can be pretty rewarding as well. Either way, it's a dish that might be outside the comfort zone of some, but very impressive to those willing to go out on a limb and try something new. I like to pair this with a crisp white wine like Sauvignon Blanc or Vinho Verde.*

| | | | | |
|---|---|---|---|---|
| 2 | pounds octopus (fresh or frozen) | | 2 | shallots |
| 2 | quarts water | | 3 | ribs celery |
| 3 | cups dry white wine | | | Plenty of sea salt (I like black lava salt for this one) |
| | Juice of 1 lemon | | | Salad mixture |
| 5 | cloves garlic | | | Southwestern Mustard Vinaigrette |

Clean the octopus well under cold water and cut away the head and beak from the tentacles. A thick ring of muscle should still attach all the tentacles. Bring all other ingredients to a simmer except the salt, then begin adding small handfuls of salt to the pot until it tastes almost as salty as the ocean.

Place the octopus tentacles in the simmering liquid, cover the pot and cook on low heat (barely simmering) for 1 to 1 1/2 hours, then remove it from the liquid.

Cover a counter surface completely with two layers of plastic wrap. Cut the 8 tentacles apart from each other, then arrange roughly in the center of the wrap. Wrap the octopus very tightly in the plastic, forming a long log shape. Tie up the ends of the plastic and place the log into a freezer overnight.

The next day, remove the plastic while the octopus is still frozen, and slice it very thinly (carpaccio) on a deli slicer. Arrange the disks around a plate, slightly overlapping each other. One thin layer is plenty. In the center of the plate, place a small amount of the salad mixture on top, then drizzle the plate with the mustard sauce and sprinkle black lava salt all over the plate to finish.

### FOR THE SALAD:

| | | | | |
|---|---|---|---|---|
| 1/4 | cup chopped black olives | | 1 | ounce micro cilantro |
| 3 | tablespoons capers | | | |

Toss together in a mixing bowl, dress lightly with the mustard vinaigrette and serve as a garnish.

### SOUTHWESTERN MUSTARD VINAIGRETTE   *Makes 1 1/3 cups*

| | | | | |
|---|---|---|---|---|
| | Juice of 4 lemons | | 1/2 | cup extra virgin olive oil |
| 2 | tablespoons Dijon mustard | | 1 | tablespoon agave nectar |
| 1/2 | teaspoon salt | | 1 1/4 | teaspoons Texas Red Dirt Rub, Southwestern Blend (see page 9) |
| 1/4 | teaspoon smoked sweet paprika | | | |

Combine all ingredients in a blender and puree until well incorporated.

# SOUPS AND SALADS

In the heat of a Texas summer, soup and salad often becomes an entire meal, especially for the business lunch or for those on the go who don't want to be bogged down by a heavy meal in the middle of the day. A seafood soup or salad is the ideal choice in many ways—high in protein and rich in flavor, but the ingredients are not necessarily "heavy" overall. A cup of spicy gumbo and a light salad with smoked shrimp is a perfect healthy choice for the workingman's lunch. Its bold flavor and generous sustenance can keep hunger away for hours.

Seafood lends itself to soups and salads in very diverse ways. Salads can be boring if they consist of mostly lettuce and dressing, but introduce smoked oysters, smoked tuna or grilled fish to the greens and a salad suddenly becomes a desirable, healthy light entrée that jumps off the menu. Soup is often called the heart of the kitchen, as it takes a little finesse and a little love to make soups that feed the soul as well as the palate. Seafood finds its way onto a menu in many ways, but the soup and salad section is one of the most popular.

# SMOKED SHRIMP OVER BABY GREENS   *Serves 14–16*

*The flavor of properly smoked shrimp is one of the most addicting things I've ever tasted. The key to making the shrimp taste great is to have the smoker at the right temperature from the beginning. A fire that's burning hot with orange or white coals puts out a very light and sweetly flavored smoke, perfect for this dish. If the wood is barely smoldering, the flavor is too sooty and tastes very strong. These shrimp work well on a light salad but also can complement many other dishes, from sandwiches*

*to casseroles. At Waters Restaurant, I garnish this salad with cucumbers, baby tomatoes and toasted pumpkin seeds.*

## FOR THE SHRIMP:

½ cup brown sugar

¼ cup salt

1 tablespoon garlic powder

1 teaspoon onion powder

½ teaspoon coriander

Pinch of cumin

2 tablespoons chile powder (I prefer Pendery's Durango blend)

1 teaspoon mustard powder

5 pounds wild shrimp, 26–30 count

2 tablespoons olive oil

Baby greens

Waters Restaurant House Dressing

Combine all dry ingredients together and whisk well. Clean and dry the shrimp, then coat with the dry rub and toss to coat thoroughly. Add the olive oil and mix one last time. Refrigerate for 20 minutes. Scatter the shrimp onto a perforated pan or wire rack, and then smoke over pecan wood for 30 minutes at 150 degrees. Check the shrimp to be sure they are cooked by cutting into one. If they have not finished cooking after 30 minutes, finish them in an oven at 350 degrees for about 4 minutes, or until cooked through. Refrigerate immediately; serve chilled.

Toss your favorite baby greens or lettuce with the dressing and top with chilled smoked shrimp.

## WATERS RESTAURANT HOUSE DRESSING   *Makes 3¼ cups*

2 paddles fresh cactus (nopales)*

5 ounces sour cream

Juice of 3 lemons

Juice of 1 lime

4 ounces fresh basil, most large stems removed

1 tablespoon Dijon mustard

2 tablespoons salt

3 cloves garlic

1 teaspoon granulated garlic

1 teaspoon onion powder

1 ounce gold tequila

½ cup olive oil

½ cup canola oil

Begin by grilling the cactus paddles over a hot fire until slightly charred on both sides and the juices begin to visibly bubble through the skin. Remove from the grill, allow to cool, and chop roughly.

Add all ingredients, except the oils, in a food processor and blend until it creates a uniform texture. Drizzle the oils in slowly while the processor is running until all of the oil is incorporated into the dressing. Refrigerate for 1 hour before using. The dressing will thicken significantly after cooling.

*\*If fresh cactus is not available, canned or jarred nopales will also work.*

# SMOKED SPICY TUNA OVER WATERCRESS   *Serves 4*

*If you don't have a smoker, this recipe can also be done on a conventional gas grill by placing wood chunks directly over the gas burners on one side and turning that side on high. Leave the other side turned off. Once the grill has filled with smoke, place the tuna over the cold side and quickly shut the lid to trap in the smoke.*

1   pound fresh Ahi (yellowfin) tuna

1   teaspoon olive oil

1   tablespoon Waters Bay Blend (see page 10)

Waters Restaurant House Dressing (see page 37)

Clean the tuna well and remove any black blood line. Rub well on all sides with olive oil and Waters Bay Blend, then refrigerate for 1 hour to allow the spices to soak in.

Prepare a smoker with pecan wood and be sure the fire is burning very hot. Once the coals have turned orange or white, the smoke will have a sweet flavor (lightly smoldering wood has a strong, sooty flavor). Place the chilled tuna on the smoker in the coolest spot, away from any direct heat. Smoke for 8–10 minutes then remove and wrap in plastic wrap; chill well. The tuna should be smoky but still very rare. Once chilled, slice the tuna into large, thin slices and arrange over watercress greens dressed lightly with Waters Restaurant House Dressing.

# SMOKED TROUT WITH MARINATED TOMATOES AND HERBS     *Serves 2–4*

*The delicate, light nature of rainbow trout really comes alive with plenty of spice and sweet smoke flavor. Rainbow trout are aquafarmed in several locations in the United States with great success. The Rushing Waters farm in Idaho is my supplier. This makes a perfect light summer lunch when great tomatoes and fresh herbs are abundant. This dish pairs perfectly with a dry rosé or medium-bodied Chardonnay.*

|   |   |
|---|---|
| 2 boneless rainbow trout fillets | 2–3 sprigs fresh tarragon |
| ½ teaspoon Waters Bay Blend (see page 10) | 1 teaspoon extra virgin olive oil |
| 3 large assorted heirloom tomatoes | Juice of 1 lemon |
| 2–3 sprigs fresh basil | Sea salt |
| 3–4 sprigs fresh oregano | Freshly ground black pepper |

Be sure the trout fillets are cleaned well of all bones. Prepare a smoker with pecan wood and be sure the fire is burning very hot. Once the coals have turned orange or white, the smoke will have a sweet flavor (lightly smoldering wood has a strong, sooty flavor). Place fillets in the smoker and cook for 15 minutes. Once cooked, allow to cool slightly, then pull off the skin and discard.

Remove the core from the tomatoes and cut into random pieces. Pick the leaves off all herbs and roughly chop together, then dress the tomatoes with the herbs, olive oil and lemon juice. Sprinkle with sea salt and pepper, and serve alongside the warm smoked trout.

# GRILLED WAHOO AND CRAB SALAD    *Serves 4–6*

*Wahoo is a richly flavored fish with a large, meaty flake that grills extremely well. I love pairing a steaky fish like wahoo with sweet and tender crab in this salad, mixed with a complex array of spices. It's fantastic when served on sourdough bread as a sandwich, as a stand-alone salad with lettuce and fresh tomatoes, or as a spread for grilled slices of bread. Swordfish will also work well in this recipe if wahoo is not available, as will opah or mahi. This dish pairs perfectly with a full-flavored Chardonnay or IPA-style beer.*

| | |
|---|---|
| 1 pound of wahoo fillet, boneless and skinless | ½ cup mayonnaise |
| ½ teaspoon Waters Bay Blend (see page 10) | ¼ teaspoon chili powder |
| | ¼ teaspoon turmeric |
| ½ teaspoon vegetable oil | Juice and zest of 1 lemon |
| 1 pound fresh lump crabmeat | 3–4 healthy dashes hot sauce |
| 1 large English cucumber, seeded and diced | 1 bunch scallions, green parts only, chopped |
| 3 ribs celery, diced | ½ teaspoon sea salt |
| 1 jalapeño pepper, seeds removed, diced | ½ teaspoon Texas Red Dirt Rub, Creole Blend (see page 9) |

Season the wahoo fillet well with Waters Bay Blend, then brush lightly with oil to prevent it from sticking to the grill. Grill over high heat for 2–3 minutes per side, until the fish is just cooked through. It's okay to leave the fish slightly on the undercooked side, but be very careful not to overcook the wahoo or it will dry out very quickly. Cook to an internal temperature of approximately 130 degrees, then remove from the grill and allow to rest for at least 5 minutes before cutting into large cubes.

Pick through the crabmeat and discard any shell pieces or cartilage, then combine the crab with the fish in a large mixing bowl. Add all remaining ingredients and mix together. Allow to sit for about 10 minutes before serving.

# CREOLE GUMBO    *Serves 10-12*

*Gumbo is a beautiful meal when served in a large bowl all by itself or the perfect beginning to almost any great dinner if served in a cup. The complexity of dark roux complemented by a variety of spices, vegetables and meats is truly good for the soul. Gumbo is a food of love—you cannot shortcut at the last minute. Either you have time to make a gumbo the right way, or you save it for another day.*

1    stick (4 ounces) butter, plus 1 ½ teaspoons, divided

5 ½    tablespoons (4 ounces) all-purpose flour

½    cup finely diced tasso

2    ribs celery, diced

1    red pepper, diced

1    green pepper, diced

1    medium yellow onion, diced

3    cloves garlic, minced

2    tablespoons Texas Red Dirt Rub, Creole Blend (see page 9)

½    cup dry white wine

2    quarts chicken stock

1 ½    cups sliced okra

Several dashes hot sauce

1    dash Worcestershire sauce

2    links smoked Andouille sausage, diced

5    ounces chicken breast, diced

6    ounces crawfish tail meat

6    ounces baby shrimp, peeled

Cooked rice for serving

Chopped green onions for garnish

Add 4 ounces butter and flour to a large pan and stir continuously over medium heat to form a roux. Cook until the roux reaches a medium caramel color. The color might be slightly darker than you are comfortable with, but a dark roux adds great depth to gumbo and is essential. The color should be somewhere between caramel candy and a Hershey bar.

Sweat the tasso, celery, peppers and onion in the roux until the vegetables are soft, adding in the garlic for the last minute or two. By this time, the roux should be dark brown. Season well with Creole Blend seasonings. Deglaze the pan with white wine while whisking, then reduce for 1 full minute. The mixture will be very thick at this point. Add chicken stock and okra. Bring to a light simmer and cook for 10 minutes. Add in the hot sauce and Worcestershire, then adjust the seasonings to your taste.

Brown the meats lightly in a separate pan along with remaining butter, then add to the mix and simmer the entire pot for approximately 15–20 minutes. Serve garnished with plain white rice and chopped green onions.

# HOME-CURED SMOKED SALMON  *Serves 8–10*

*It takes time and several processes to make your own smoked salmon at home, but the final product is a beautiful thing to be proud of. King salmon or silver salmon are my favorite varieties to use for cold smoking, but most species of salmon can work well. One of the keys to cold smoking is to get the flavor of smoke without cooking the fish with heat. One way to accomplish this is to place the salmon directly over a tray of ice and just under another tray of ice to keep it cool while it absorbs the smoke. I prefer pecan, oak or hickory wood for this technique. After smoking, the salmon must rest overnight before slicing; otherwise, it will seem very strong and intense on the smoke flavor.*

*I generally smoke this salmon for about 2 hours, but 1–4 hours is the acceptable range. It's worth experimenting to find your favorite level of smoke and what type of wood you like best. Remember that the coals need to be burning hot (white or orange) for a sweet smoke flavor, but the smoker temperature needs to be cool.*

| | |
|---|---|
| 1 whole side of salmon, skin on | 7 tablespoons brown sugar |
| 1 ounce bourbon (I prefer Firestone & Robertson) | 1 bunch fresh dill |
| Zest of 2 lemons | Cucumber slaw (see page 182) |
| 5 tablespoons kosher salt | Lemon wedges |
| | Toasted bread |

Clean the salmon fillet well and remove any pin bones and scales. Pat dry with a paper towel. Liberally brush the bourbon over the flesh side of the salmon, then refrigerate, uncovered, while preparing the rest of the ingredients.

Mix the zest, salt and sugar to make the cure mixture. Lay a large layer of plastic wrap or parchment paper down on a sheet pan and place about half of the cure mix down in a similar shape as the salmon fillet. Lay the salmon skin-side down on top of the cure, then thickly and evenly cover the top of the salmon with the remaining cure. Layer the dill thinly over the top of the salmon. Place another layer of plastic over the top, and set another sheet pan on top and weigh it down with a few canned goods to keep it firmly in place. Allow the salmon to cure, lightly pressed, in the refrigerator overnight.

On the second day, remove the fish and rinse lightly under cold water. Pat dry, then place in a cold smoker (a smoker that doesn't get over 100 degrees). Allow the salmon to smoke for 1–4 hours, depending on how much smoke flavor you like, without letting the temperature get over 100 degrees inside. Remove salmon from the smoker, wrap it in plastic and cool overnight in the fridge.

Slice salmon very thinly with a sharp knife. Serve over cucumber slaw with lemon wedges and toasted bread.

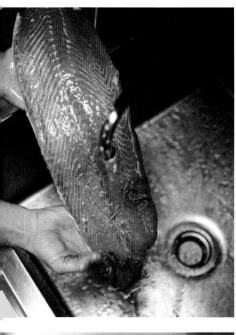

# LOBSTER AND SHRIMP BISQUE   *Serves 6-8*

*Nothing is quite as rich and decadent as a bisque. It's hearty enough to be an entire meal when paired with a crusty bread. The addition of cognac right before serving really sets off the flavors well, giving a sweet and slightly smoky background to the soup. Be sure not to cook the lobster and shrimp too long, or their texture will become tough and stringy. Simmering for just a minute right at the end should be enough to get them tender and succulent.*

| | | | |
|---|---|---|---|
| 1 | live lobster (1 ½-pound range) | 1 | tablespoon tomato paste |
| 1 | pound raw shrimp, heads and shells on | ½ | cup white wine |
| 2 | leeks, washed thoroughly and diced | 3 | ounces cognac |
| 2 | ribs celery, diced | 4 | cups heavy cream |
| 1 | shallot, diced | 1 | cup water |
| 1 | small carrot, peeled and diced | 4–6 | stems parsley |
| 3 | cloves garlic, minced | 2 | bay leaves |
| 4 | tablespoons (½ stick) butter | 1 | teaspoon kosher salt |
| | | ¼ | teaspoon freshly ground black pepper |

Boil the lobster in water for approximately 3 minutes, then remove and place in cold water until cool enough to handle. Boil the whole shrimp (heads and all) for 1 ½ minutes, then remove to cold water as well. Remove the claw meat and tail meat from the lobster, chop into large pieces and reserve for later. Reserve the shells and the tamale (the green liver of the lobster), but discard all of the other organs. Peel the shrimp and remove the heads and veins, but reserve the heads and shells. If the shrimp are very large, cut in half or thirds and reserve the meat for later.

In a heavy-bottomed soup pot, sauté the leeks, celery, shallot, carrot and garlic in butter until soft. Add the reserved lobster shells, shrimp shells and tamale, plus the tomato paste and white wine. Reduce the wine slowly until the pan is almost dry, then add in the cognac and flame. The shells should singe a bit around the edges. When the flame goes out, add in the cream and water and bring to a simmer. Tie the parsley stems and bay leaves together with a piece of string so they may be removed easily later, and place in the pot. Cover and simmer gently for approximately 15–20 minutes. Remove the parsley and bay leaves, season with salt and pepper and puree with a stick blender as much as possible; some of the shells will not puree completely, and that is okay. Strain the mixture through a fine mesh chinois or cheesecloth to remove any shell particles.

Return the strained soup to the pot, taste it and adjust seasonings one last time, if needed. Add the reserved lobster and shrimp meat, simmer for 1 minute to finish cooking the meat, and add a few drops of cognac to finish right before serving.

# CREAMY CLAM CHOWDER   *Serves 10-12*

*Often referred to as New England–style clam chowder, the creamy variations are extremely hearty and rich. The key to this chowder is plenty of really good clams. Typically, quahog clams or cherrystone clams are the best for chowder, since they are larger and yield more meat for the buck. Chop the meat roughly before using these clams if you buy them whole. Freshly chopped clams can save you some time and energy and are usually pretty easy to find at most fishmongers, but using canned clams is a decent substitute and will save some money.*

| | |
|---|---|
| 6 ounces bacon, diced | 1 cup milk |
| 2 tablespoons butter | 1 pound Yukon gold potatoes, peeled and diced |
| 4 shallots, diced | 2–3 dashes hot sauce |
| 1 poblano pepper, diced | 2–3 dashes Worcestershire sauce |
| 2 leeks, white parts only, cleaned well and chopped | 2 pounds chopped fresh clams or 8 (6 ½-ounce) cans clams with liquid reserved (if using canned, separate juice and reserve for use in place of clam juice) |
| 2 cloves garlic, minced | |
| 4 tablespoons all-purpose flour | |
| ⅓ cup dry white wine | 1 teaspoon salt |
| 1 quart clam juice | Crackers |
| 1 pint heavy cream | |

Begin by rendering out most of the fat from the bacon in a soup pot. Remove the bacon just before it gets crispy and reserve for later. To the same pot, add the butter, then sauté the shallots, pepper, leeks and garlic until slightly soft. Sprinkle in the flour and stir quickly to incorporate it into the butter; cook for 2–3 minutes, without letting the flour brown. Deglaze the pan with white wine and allow to reduce slightly. Add the clam juice (if using canned clams, use their liquid as part of the total clam juice), cream, milk and potatoes; bring to a simmer. Season with a few heavy shakes of hot sauce and Worcestershire sauce, and simmer lightly until the potatoes are cooked, roughly 15 minutes. Add the bacon and chopped clams to the pot, and simmer an additional 8–10 minutes. Add the salt, adjust to taste, and serve with crackers.

# LITTLENECK CLAM CHOWDER WITH TOMATOES  *Serves 6-8*

*This chowder version more closely resembles a Manhattan-style clam chowder than the creamy variety. What makes this chowder superb is using plenty of live littleneck clams. The canned clams add to the overall body, but live clams are also a must. They do need a good scrubbing before they can be used but are well worth the effort for a dish like this. Topneck clams, mahogany clams or even cockles can be used as a substitution in this dish, but I prefer the perfectly sized littlenecks if they are available.*

- 3 thick slices bacon, diced
- 1 tablespoon olive oil
- 1 small onion, diced
- 1 Anaheim pepper, diced
- 3 ribs celery, diced
- 2 cloves garlic, minced
- 1 small Yukon gold potato, diced
- 1 ounce dry vermouth
- 1 bay leaf
- Pinch of celery seed
- Pinch of dried thyme
- Pinch of dried parsley
- Pinch of sweet paprika
- 2 cups clam juice
- 1 15-ounce can tomato puree or plain tomato sauce
- 1 6 1/2-ounce can baby clams
- 1 14 1/2-ounce can chopped tomatoes
- 1 teaspoon sea salt
- 1/2 teaspoon freshly ground black pepper
- 3 dozen live littleneck clams

Begin by rendering the bacon in a heavy-bottomed soup pot. Just before the bacon gets crispy remove it from the pot and reserve. To the same pot, add the olive oil and sauté the onion, pepper, celery and garlic just until soft. Add all remaining ingredients, except the live clams, and bring to a simmer. Cover and simmer lightly for 20 minutes, until the potatoes are cooked through.

Scrub the live clams well under cold water to remove any grit from the outside of the shell, then add them to the pot. Simmer for roughly 8 minutes, until the clams have all opened. If any clams do not open after 8 minutes, pull them out and discard. Remove the bay leaf and serve with plenty of whole clams in each bowl.

# GULF SEAFOOD STEW   *Serves 10–12*

*I listed redfish, shrimp and crab as my favorite blend for this soup, but a good seafood stew is made from whatever is really fresh at the time. Snapper, grouper, sheepshead, triggerfish, cobia and even oysters can work well; check the fishmonger's selection. The key to this soup is to begin with a rich base, properly seasoned, and then add in the great fresh fish.*

## FOR THE BASE:

| | |
|---|---|
| 1 | white onion, small dice |
| 1 | poblano pepper, small dice |
| 1 | jalapeño pepper, small dice (seeds optional) |
| 1 | red bell pepper, small dice |
| 3 | ribs celery, small dice |
| 1/2 | cup diced carrot |
| 5 | cloves garlic, minced |
| 2 | tablespoons olive oil |
| 1 1/2 | cups white wine |

| | |
|---|---|
| 10 | Roma tomatoes, finely diced (to make 2 1/2 cups) |
| 2 | 14 1/2-ounce cans diced tomatoes |
| 24 | ounces clam juice |
| 2 | teaspoons chipotle puree (canned chipotles in adobo pureed together until smooth) |
| 2 | tablespoons chopped fresh parsley |
| 3 | tablespoons chopped fresh thyme |
| 3 | tablespoons chopped fresh oregano |
| | Salt, optional |

## FOR THE SEAFOOD:

| | |
|---|---|
| 12 | ounces redfish fillet, large dice |
| 1 | pound shrimp, 21–25 count, peeled and deveined |

| | |
|---|---|
| 1 | pound lump crabmeat (picked through for shell pieces) |

In a large soup pot, sauté the onion, peppers, celery, carrots and garlic in olive oil until soft. Deglaze with the white wine and reduce by half. Add the chopped tomatoes, canned tomatoes and clam juice, and simmer together for 15 minutes. Finish the base by adding the chipotle puree and fresh herbs. Depending on which clam juice you use, it may be necessary to adjust the seasoning with salt. Some clam juice products are already quite salty, so be sure to taste it first to see if additional salt is needed.

Once the soup base has simmered for 3–4 minutes, gently add in the seafood and give one gentle stir. Simmer lightly, covered, for 10–12 minutes, until all fish is cooked through, then taste for seasonings one last time. Do not overstir the soup or the crab pieces and fish will break apart.

# WHOLE ARTICHOKES STUFFED WITH SHRIMP SALAD *Serves 4*

*This shrimp salad is fantastic on its own or sandwiched between slices of toasted bread with crisp lettuce or arugula. The combination of chilled shrimp with steamed artichokes really screams out "summer" to me. I like to pair this dish with a light Riesling or Pilsner-style beer.*

*Be sure to mix the shrimp salad at the last minute so it doesn't get watery. Over time, the salt in the salad pulls water out of the shrimp and causes it to pool up.*

| | |
|---|---|
| 4 large globe artichokes | 1–2 dashes hot sauce |
| 1 pound cooked Gulf shrimp, 26–30 count | 3 tablespoons red bell pepper, finely diced |
| 2 tablespoons mayonnaise | 2 tablespoons chopped fresh chives |
| Juice of 1 small lemon | 3 tablespoons diced cucumber |
| 1/2 teaspoon Texas Red Dirt Rub, 100 (see page 9) | 3 tablespoons diced celery |
| | Pinch of dry mustard powder |

Prepare a steamer large enough to fit the artichokes and preheat the water with the lid on. Trim the artichoke stems up to the base so they can sit flat once cooked. With a serrated knife, cut the tops off the artichokes about 2 inches down from the tallest leaf. Once trimmed, place very quickly into the steamer and cover. Steam for approximately 40 minutes, or until the hearts are tender. Remove and chill in the refrigerator. Once cooled, scoop out the inside of the artichokes with a spoon, removing the thistles but leaving the hearts intact.

Combine the shrimp with all remaining ingredients in a large mixing bowl and toss well to combine. Scoop a large helping of the shrimp salad into the center of each artichoke and serve chilled.

# POACHED OR STEAMED

Poaching and steaming are two of the most gentle and respectful ways to prepare seafood. Both techniques work well for even the most delicate of fish. All types of shellfish (crustaceans and mollusks) react well to steaming and poaching, as do most finfish. Simply treating fresh seafood to a gentle and moist heated environment typically retains the most original and authentic seafood flavors.

Typically, poaching (in liquid below the boiling point) is the gentlest approach to cooking fish if the temperature of the liquid doesn't rise above 180 degrees. One of the greatest benefits of poaching is the ability to get the fish cooked to the proper degree of doneness with very little guesswork. Although poaching is a delicate approach, it can be monitored closely with a thermometer, giving the cook an easy opportunity to pull the fish from the poaching liquid at exactly the right moment. The other beautiful aspect of poaching is its ability to impart subtle flavors and nuances through the flavorful poaching liquid. White wine, vermouth, peppercorns, lemon and herbs are fantastic flavors that work very well in poaching liquid, imposing a hint of their complementary flavors.

Steaming is one of the most basic and possibly most common approaches to cooking many types of seafood, especially shellfish. My personal choice for the ultimate lobster experience is unadulterated, straightforward steamed lobster; I find that steaming preserves more of the natural flavor than boiling. The temperature inside a steam pot is very constant, so steaming provides uniform cooking. I often use a steaming technique to quickly cook mussels, clams or oysters that might later be used for something else since it imparts no other flavors and cooks very consistently.

# STEAMED CLAMS IN GARLIC BUTTER *Serves 2*

*Steamed clams are a true comfort food for many people—simple and quick to prepare and perfect with a hot, crusty loaf of sourdough bread for sopping up extra sauce. There is a fantastic mussel/clam pot made of cast iron that I love to use for this dish, but a simple sauté pan gets the job done just as easily. If you don't have a good lid for your sauté pan, place another sauté pan upside down on top to trap in the steam while the clams cook. Littlenecks are my favorite, but cherrystone, top neck, mahogany clams or even cockles work well with this preparation.*

- 2  pounds live clams
- 3  tablespoons butter
- 4  cloves garlic, minced
- 2  tablespoons chopped flat leaf parsley
- 1  tablespoon chopped cilantro

Pinch of hot smoked paprika

Juice of 1 small lemon

- 1  ounce white wine
- 1  ounce dry vermouth

Wash and scrub the clams under cold water to remove any grit from their shells. Set aside.

In a heavy-bottomed pot, melt the butter and sauté the garlic until it begins to soften, but do not let it brown. Add remaining ingredients, except for the clams, and simmer for 2 full minutes. Then add all the clams to the pot. Cover and steam until the shells open, roughly 5–6 minutes. Discard any that refuse to open. Serve hot with the broth and plenty of crusty bread for dipping.

# STEAMED MUSSELS WITH JALAPEÑO    *Serves 1–2*

*This is one of the fastest and easiest preparations to pull off in a hurry, yet the presentation makes it look like you've done a great deal of work. Before cooking, be sure to clean the mussels well and discard any that are not still alive. (If a mussel shell is open before cooking, tap on the shell; if it does not close, discard it.) I love the lightly spicy broth that this dish makes almost as much as the sweet mussels themselves.*

| | | | |
|---|---|---|---|
| 1 | pound live mussels | 2 | ounces heavy cream |
| 2 | cloves garlic, minced | 1 | Roma tomato, seeded and diced |
| 2 | large jalapeños, seeded and diced | | Juice of 1 lime |
| 1 | tablespoon butter | 1 | teaspoon chopped fresh cilantro |
| 1 | ounce dry white wine | ¼ | teaspoon kosher salt |

Clean the mussels one at a time by rinsing and pulling off any beard that might be attached. The beard is nothing more than the part of the mussel that attaches itself to the ropes that most mussels are grown on. Sometimes they still have a small piece of that rope fiber attached. If any seaweed or barnacles are attached, try to remove as much as possible. Set the mussels aside.

In a medium-sized pot, sauté the garlic and jalapeños in butter for 1 minute. Add the white wine and cream and bring to a simmer. Add remaining ingredients, including mussels; stir once and then cover with a lid. Simmer for 2 minutes, or until the mussels have all opened. (Pull out and discard any that refuse to open.) Serve immediately with crusty bread for dipping.

# POACHED SALMON WITH COOL CUCUMBER SAUCE   *Serves 8–10*

*This poached dish is one of the best ways to enjoy the true flavor of wild salmon. I prefer making it with wild Alaskan salmon for the best flavor and overall health benefits, although other parts of the world can also produce great salmon. (I recommend avoiding the bargain brand Atlantic salmon at big-box stores, as its flavor, health benefits and environmental impact are quite poor by comparison.) This is an excellent dish to serve cold in the center of the table, family style, with a chilled bottle of Sauvignon Blanc or Pinot Grigio.*

| | | | |
|---|---|---|---|
| 2 | cups dry white wine | 3 | tablespoons whole black peppercorns |
| 1 | lemon, halved | 5 | cloves garlic |
| 2 | ribs celery, roughly chopped | 2 | teaspoons salt |
| 4 | cups cold water | | 12- to 16-ounce fillet of salmon (I prefer wild Alaskan king or silver salmon) |
| 10 | bay leaves | | |

Combine all ingredients, except fish, in a large saucepot and bring to a simmer. Allow to simmer together for 10 minutes, then reduce the temperature to approximately 180 degrees. Carefully lower the salmon into the hot liquid and cook for about 5 minutes. Test the salmon with a thermometer to be sure it's cooked through. The internal temperature should be 125–130 degrees for medium rare, which is my preferred temperature for salmon, or up to 140 for medium. The cooking time may vary slightly, depending on the thickness of the fish. Using a large slotted fish spatula, carefully remove the salmon from the poaching liquid and place on a dinner plate. (This can be served warm or chilled (my preference). Serve with various crackers, lemon wedges, Cool Cucumber Sauce, and Jicama and Citrus Slaw (see page 182).

## COOL CUCUMBER SAUCE   *Makes 3 cups*

| | | | |
|---|---|---|---|
| 1 | English cucumber, peeled and seeded | 1 1/2 | tablespoons chopped fresh dill |
| 8 | ounces plain Greek yogurt | 1 | tablespoon chopped fresh chives |
| 8 | ounces sour cream | 1 1/2 | teaspoons chopped fresh mint |
| 1 | clove garlic, minced | | Pinch of cayenne pepper |
| | Juice of 1/2 lemon | 1/2 | teaspoon salt |
| | | 1/2 | teaspoon cracked black pepper |

Chop the cucumber into medium dice, then combine all ingredients in a mixing bowl and whisk together. Refrigerate for at least 1 hour before serving.

# Steamed Lobster with Lemon and Red Chile Butter   *Serves 2*

*I love the rich, intense flavor of succulent lobster meat paired with a tiny a hint of spice and complexity. This is a recipe best served family style, the kind of meal that can be eaten with your hands. The red chile butter is also fantastic spread across grilled corn on the cob or sopped up with dense bread. When it comes to the decadence of whole lobsters, pass out the bibs, set out plenty of paper towels and get your hands a little dirty. It's worth the mess.*

2   live lobsters (1 ½ pounds each)

Prepare a steamer large enough to fit both lobsters and heat fully. Place both lobsters in the steamer and cover with a lid. Steam for 12 minutes, then remove and serve whole with warm Red Chile Butter for dipping.

## Red Chile Butter

1   red bell pepper

8   tablespoons (1 stick) salted butter, softened

¼   teaspoon cayenne pepper

⅛   teaspoon chipotle powder

Pinch of sea salt

Pinch of chile powder (I prefer Pendery's El Rey)

¼   teaspoon granulated garlic

Juice of ½ lemon

Roast the bell pepper over an open flame until black on all sides. A gas burner on your stovetop or a very hot grill works well for this. Once blackened, place pepper in a paper sack or zip lock bag to sweat for 10 minutes, until cool enough to handle. Scrape off the black skins with the back side of a knife blade, then remove all seeds and the stem. Place the roasted red pepper in a food processor, add remaining ingredients, and blend until smooth. Serve warm with steamed lobster.

# SHALLOW-POACHED TROUT WITH WHITE WINE AND HERBS *Serves 2*

*This dish works well with speckled trout from the Gulf or freshwater rainbow trout. In either case, the trout should be boneless and skinless to start. The delicate and light nature of trout is perfect for this kind of dish, whose flavors pair perfectly with Chablis or other unoaked chardonnay. I also love the idea of cooking a one-pan dish with very little cleanup required.*

| | | | | |
|---|---|---|---|---|
| 1/2 | cup white wine | | 2 | 8-ounce trout fillets |
| 4 | tablespoons heavy cream | | 1/2 | teaspoon chopped fresh tarragon |
| 1 | shallot, sliced | | 1/2 | teaspoon chopped fresh dill |
| 1 | clove garlic, minced | | 1/2 | teaspoon chopped fresh basil |
| | Juice of 1 small lemon | | 1/4 | teaspoon sea salt |

Place the wine, cream, shallot, garlic and lemon in a sauté pan and bring to a light simmer. Gently lay the trout in and continue to simmer lightly just until the delicate fillets are cooked through, about 6–7 minutes. Once they are cooked, carefully remove the fish from the pan with a slotted fish spatula and place on a warm dinner plate or platter. Reduce the liquid in the pan until it barely starts to thicken, then add in the fresh herbs and salt and simmer for 1 more minute. To serve, pour the contents of the pan over the warm trout fillets.

# BRAIDED POACHED ARCTIC CHAR  *Serves 4*

*Arctic char is a fish in the salmon family, with an extremely mild flavor and delicate flake. Char live in cold, clean, fresh water, like the rivers in Alaska, but also are available from several aquafarms. I tend not to like most aquafarms, in general, but the Icelandic aquacultured char is an outstanding product that I recommend wholeheartedly. This dish seems fancy but is not very difficult to pull off. It's truly a visual showstopper and extremely healthy. The fish can easily be cooked without braiding and the flavor will be the same, but sometimes it's fun to show off a touch.*

| | |
|---|---|
| 16  ounces Arctic char fillets, boneless and skinless | 1  large head butter lettuce |
| 4  scallions | Waters House Dressing (see page 37) |

Blanch the scallions in boiling water for 1 minute, until they are soft enough to be used as ties for the fish. Cut the Arctic char into long strips, roughly 1 inch wide, to be poached later. Sixteen ounces of char should yield enough for roughly 12 strips, but the thickness of the fish may vary. Braid 3 strips together at a time, yielding 4 braided portions overall. Tie each end of the braided fish with blanched scallions to keep them from coming undone when cooking. Set aside and keep chilled while preparing the poaching liquid.

## FOR THE POACHING LIQUID:

| | |
|---|---|
| 2  quarts water | 3  tablespoons whole black peppercorns |
| 2  cups dry white wine | |
| Juice of 4 lemons | 8  cloves fresh garlic |
| 6  bay leaves | 1/3  cup sea salt |

In a large pot bring all ingredients to a boil and cook for 6–8 minutes. Reduce to just below the simmering point, where the water is very hot but not bubbling. This is usually around 180 degrees, depending on your altitude (at higher altitudes, water boils at a slightly lower temperature). Very gently, lower the braided char into the liquid and cook for 5–6 minutes, keeping a careful eye on the temperature of the cooking liquid to keep it hot but not bubbling. Once cooked, remove the fish carefully with a slotted fish spatula and place on a dinner plate to rest. Cut the butter lettuce into thick strips and toss with the dressing. Divide the salad evenly among four plates and then plate then place the warm, braided char on top, drizzling with a touch of extra dressing to finish.

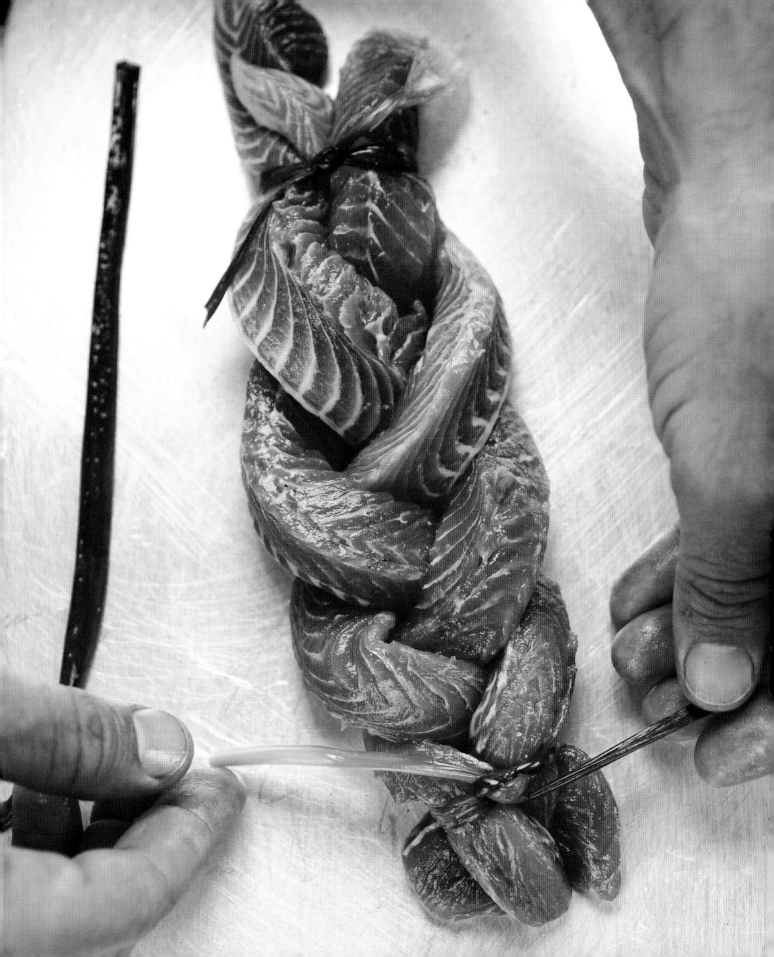

# OLIVE OIL–POACHED SHRIMP WITH LEMON-BASIL VINAIGRETTE *Serves 4*

*Poaching shrimp in olive oil is a good way to retain all of the flavor and moistness of the shrimp while also imparting a slight acidic and peppery component. Once the shrimp have been drained from the oil, their texture is perfect and not at all oily. This is perhaps my favorite method for truly fresh shrimp. It's light and healthy and showcases the natural flavor of the shrimp with a light dressing to complement the dish. Be sure to use wild-caught domestic shrimp for best flavor and quality.*

| | |
|---|---|
| 1 pound domestic wild-caught raw shrimp, peeled and deveined (tails optional) | 1/2 teaspoon freshly ground black pepper |
| 1 teaspoon sea salt | 4 cups olive oil |
| | Arugula |
| | Lemon-Basil Vinaigrette |

Season shrimp with the salt and pepper and allow to sit for 5 minutes.

Add the olive oil to a deep pot and bring the temperature to 180 degrees. Gently drop the shrimp into the oil and cook for 7 minutes, until they are pink and opaque. The time may vary slightly, depending on the size of the shrimp, so pull one out and cut it to see if the center is cooked through. Remove shrimp from the oil and place in a strainer or colander set over a container to drain off excess oil.

Once shrimp have cooled slightly, serve over arugula drizzled with Lemon Basil Vinaigrette.

## LEMON-BASIL VINAIGRETTE *Makes 1 cup*

| | |
|---|---|
| 18–20 large leaves of fresh basil | 1/4 teaspoon sea salt |
| 1 1/2 tablespoons Dijon mustard | 1/4 teaspoon granulated garlic |
| 4 teaspoons lemon juice | 1 tablespoon chopped capers |
| 3/4 cup extra virgin olive oil | Pinch of freshly ground black pepper |

Blanch the basil leaves in simmering water for 15–20 seconds, then remove from the water and place directly in a blender. Add remaining ingredients and pulse until the dressing is smooth and creamy.

# SHALLOW-POACHED POMPANO WITH CAPERS AND OLIVES *Serves 2*

*Shallow poaching is an easy and fantastic way to keep mess to a minimum and flavors to a maximum. It requires only one pan from start to finish, and the sauce is a rich reduction of the entire poaching contents. The acidic and briny characteristics of this sauce complement the pompano very well and can be paired perfectly with a dry rosé wine or even a light Pinot Noir or Chianti.*

| | | | |
|---|---|---|---|
| 1 | 14-ounce can diced tomatoes, with juice | ½ | cup dry white wine |
| 6–8 | pitted black olives, sliced | 2 | 6- to 8-ounce pompano fillets, boneless, skinless |
| 6–8 | pitted green olives, sliced | 6–8 | sprigs fresh flat-leaf parsley, chopped |
| 3 | cloves garlic, minced | 2–3 | sprigs fresh oregano, chopped |
| 2 | tablespoons chopped capers | | |

Add tomatoes, olives, garlic, capers and wine to a sauté pan and bring to a light simmer. Once simmering, gently slide the fish fillets into the pan and simmer for about 7 minutes, depending on the thickness of the pompano. Once cooked through, remove the fillets carefully with a slotted fish spatula and place on a warm dinner plate or platter. Reduce the tomato mixture until slightly thick, then pour the entire contents of the pan over the pompano. Garnish with freshly chopped parsley and oregano just before serving.

# SAUTÉED OR PAN SEARED

As a technique, sautéing is probably the most universally accepted and most widely used method for cooking a fish fillet. Most fish really benefit from being seared a dark golden brown and crusty on at least one side of the fillet. When proteins are caramelized (browned), they usually take on more in-depth and complex flavors. The technique is simple if a few basic principles are followed:

For both pan searing and sautéing, always begin by heating a pan. While the pan is heating, check to be sure the fish is not too wet on the surface; blot the fillets dry with paper towels.

Once the pan is heated, add a touch of oil (or other fat) to the pan and tilt it to completely coat the bottom.

Within a few seconds of adding in the oil, gently place the fish in the pan, laying it in a direction away from you to avoid getting splattered. (If the pan is heated properly, the fish will immediately begin to sizzle and pop. If nothing happens when the fish hits the pan, it's not hot enough; remove the fish and wait until the oil is hot.) As soon as the fish hits the hot pan, give the pan a brisk little shake back and forth to ensure the fish isn't sticking to the pan. Once the surface of the fish starts to caramelize, there shouldn't be any problem with sticking, even in a pan lacking a nonstick surface.

The basic difference between sautéing and pan searing is that in sautéing, the food is cooked on the stovetop, while in pan-searing, the food gets a golden sear on the stovetop and then goes into the oven for further cooking. This chapter covers all of my favorite seafood dishes that generally get cooked on the stovetop to one degree or another.

# HERB-CRUSTED SHEEPSHEAD   *Serves 2*

*Sheepshead is an underutilized fish from the Gulf, often caught around bridge pilings and in the bays. These fish have huge teeth and a strange look, but their flesh is extremely mild and flaky, taking well to the flavor of bright, fresh herbs. Typically, it's a budget-friendly fish as well. Snapper, grouper and redfish are good substitutes, but it's worth seeking out sheepshead when possible. The wise angler often heads to the bridges and bays for these fish when the seas are too rough to head offshore to deeper water.*

1   tablespoon chopped fresh basil

1   tablespoon chopped fresh parsley

1   teaspoon chopped fresh dill

1   teaspoon chopped fresh tarragon

1   teaspoon sea salt

Pinch of freshly ground black pepper

2   6- to 8-ounce fillets of sheepshead, boneless and skinless

2   teaspoons olive oil

Warm German-Style Potato Salad, for serving (see page 190)

1   tablespoon butter

Juice of 1 lemon

Preheat oven to 375 degrees.

Combine all the fresh herbs, salt and pepper together and scatter across a large dinner plate. Pat the fish dry with paper towels, then press the fillets down into the herbs to heavily coat them on both sides.

Heat the olive oil in a medium-hot, ovenproof, nonstick sauté pan and lightly sear the fish for 1–2 minutes on the first side. Turn the fillets over, then place the entire pan into preheated oven and finish cooking for approximately 8 minutes, depending on the thickness of your fish.

Spoon Warm German-Style Potato Salad onto two dinner plates. Remove fish from the oven and place fillets atop the salad. Melt the butter in the still-hot pan. Add the lemon juice, season lightly with a touch of salt and pepper and pour over the herb-crusted fish to finish.

# Seared Scallops with White Bean Puree and Dill Beurre Blanc *Serves 5*

*Scallops are one of the few seafood items that can be found all year long. Not all scallops are created equally however, so get to know your fishmonger to get the best varieties. Diver scallops tend to be the best selection; always ask for dry-packed scallops, never wet-packed, as wet means that they have been packed in a solution to make them last longer. My single favorite scallop in the sea is called the Mano de León (paw of the lion) and is hand harvested from the waters of Baja. Nothing beats the sweet flavor and huge size of these prized beauties.*

*The most important thing to remember when searing scallops is to get them well browned (caramelized) on each side to bring out their best flavor.*

| | |
|---|---|
| 1 | pound great northern beans (white beans) |
| 1 | small onion, diced |
| 2 | cloves garlic, whole |
| 1 | quart chicken stock |
| 1 | pasilla chile, stem and seeds removed |
| 1 | teaspoon salt |
| 4 | tablespoons olive oil |

| | |
|---|---|
| 15 | large diver scallops |
| | Freshly ground black pepper |
| 1 1/2 | tablespoons clarified butter (ghee)* |
| 1 | shallot, minced |
| | Splash of dry white wine |
| | Juice of 2 lemons |
| 2 | tablespoons heavy cream |
| 4–6 | tablespoons cold butter |
| 1 1/2 | tablespoons chopped fresh dill |

*For the beans:* Soak the white beans in a pot of cold water overnight, then drain in a colander and rinse under cold water. In another pot, sauté onion and garlic until soft. Add the chicken stock, pasilla chile and beans, and simmer until beans are tender, approximately 70–90 minutes. Drain off most of the cooking liquid, leaving about 1/2 cup in the pot. Add the salt then puree the entire mixture with a stick blender until smooth. Drizzle in the olive oil while pureeing to add a nice texture and depth of flavor. If the mixture is too thick, thin down with a little more of the cooking liquid. If too thin, simmer on low until it reduces and thickens. Adjust seasoning to taste; cover and set aside until ready to serve.

*For the scallops:* Clean the scallops and pat dry with a paper towel, then season on both sides with salt and pepper. Heat a large nonstick pan until almost smoking. Drizzle in clarified butter and brown the scallops on both sides over high heat. It's very important to cook the scallops until well browned on each side. They should be turned only one time. If the pan is not large enough to fit the scallops without them touching each other, cook in batches, but do not overcrowd the pan. Remove the scallops and set aside on a warm plate.

Add chopped shallot to the hot pan and sauté quickly. Deglaze with a splash of white wine and the lemon juice. Reduce by at least half, then add the heavy cream and reduce until it thickens. Reduce heat to low. When the sauce has quit bubbling, add the cold butter in chunks and swirl the pan to incorporate the butter into the sauce. When all of the butter is incorporated, add the fresh dill, then immediately remove pan from heat and check for seasonings. This sauce will not hold for long, so serve immediately. Place the scallops on a layer of the bean puree and pour the fresh pan sauce right over the top.

*In a heavy-bottomed saucepot, cook unsalted butter on medium heat until it begins to boil. Once the butter begins to boil, it will soon separate into the oil (or solids) and water, which will end up at the bottom of the pot. Turn the heat to low and cook until solids begin to rise to the top and foam. Watch the mixture and remove from heat once all of the liquid (which has separated to the bottom) has evaporated. The butter is done when no more steam rises from it, but be careful not to cook too long or the butter will begin to brown. Pour the hot butter through a fine-meshed strainer lined with cheesecloth. The bright yellow oil from the butter will yield approximately 75 percent of the amount that you started with. For 1 pound of whole butter, 12 ounces of clarified butter may be extracted.*

# SHRIMP CREOLE   *Serves 5–6*

*Shrimp creole is a dish close to my heart. Anyone who has ever lived in or near New Orleans can smell a good shrimp creole from two blocks away. My version leans slightly more Texas than Louisiana, but we've always been very neighborly between the two states, lending back and forth with ease. The key to great shrimp creole is, of course, great shrimp. Use the best quality, wild-caught Gulf shrimp that you can find. White shrimp is my favorite for this dish but brown, pink or royal red will also work. Imported shrimp will not have anywhere near the same quality or taste as what our fishermen pull from the Gulf.*

- 3  tablespoons butter
- 2  tablespoons all-purpose flour
- 1  small yellow onion, medium dice
- 1  red bell pepper, medium dice
- 1  poblano pepper, medium dice
- 2  jalapeño peppers, fine dice (seeds optional)
- 3  ribs celery, medium dice
- 4  cloves garlic, minced
- 2  cups shrimp stock or chicken stock
- 1  28-ounce can chopped tomatoes

- 1  tablespoon Texas Red Dirt Rub, Creole Blend (see page 9)
- 2–3  dashes Worcestershire sauce
- 4–5  dashes hot sauce
- 1  pound shrimp, peeled and deveined (tails optional)
- Juice of 1 lime
- ½  bunch fresh cilantro, chopped
- Cooked white rice
- 1  bunch green onions, green parts only, chopped

In a large saucepan, begin by adding the butter and flour and bringing to medium-high heat. Stir together for about 2 minutes, just until the roux (mixture of butter and flour) begins to bubble and smell like sourdough toast, but do not brown. Add the onion, peppers and celery and cook for 2–3 minutes, until the vegetables begin to slightly soften, then add in the garlic and continue to cook for 1 more minute. Add the stock and whisk until the flour has incorporated into the liquid and no lumps remain. Add the tomato, season with the Creole Blend and add the Worcestershire sauce and hot sauce. Bring to a simmer and cook for 15 minutes. Add the shrimp, lime and cilantro and simmer together in the sauce for 2–3 minutes until the shrimp have just cooked through. This time may vary, depending on the size of shrimp that you choose, but be careful not to overcook your shrimp or they will become tough and dry. Serve over white rice and garnish with freshly chopped green onions.

# CLAM AND PANCETTA DIP    *Serves 8–10*

*I have to admit that I first created this dish while watching an episode of* The Restaurant *with the staff of my first restaurant. We all gathered weekly to watch the reality show and I typically fixed a few appetizers. The previous episode had featured the celebrity chef screaming at the top of his lungs, "Where the &\*%# are my CLAMS," over and over in the kitchen. So my dish became known around work as the Where the &\*%# are my Clams Dip. It's been a party favorite for years now, and I make it for every type of occasion, from Super Bowl parties to backyard barbecues. Clams are easy to find year-round and, in a pinch, the canned stuff will work. Even my kids eat clams when I make a dip out of them, though I won't tell them the real name till they are quite a bit older.*

| | |
|---|---|
| 4 ounces pancetta, finely diced | ¼ teaspoon cayenne pepper |
| 1 shallot, minced | ½ teaspoon Worcestershire sauce |
| 2 cloves garlic, minced | Juice of 1 lemon |
| 2 tablespoons white wine | 4 ounces (½ brick) cream cheese |
| 8 ounces chopped clams | 4 ounces Boursin cheese |
| ½ teaspoon chopped fresh thyme | Salt and freshly ground black pepper |

In a large sauté pan begin by rendering the fat from the pancetta over medium heat, until the pancetta is almost crisp; then remove meat from the pan, leaving the fat. Add the shallot and garlic and sweat until the shallots are soft and translucent. Deglaze with white wine. Add the clams and simmer until the pan is almost dry. Add all remaining ingredients, including the pancetta, and cook gently for 2–3 minutes, or until the cheese has melted. Serve with flatbreads or crackers for dipping.

# RED SNAPPER VERACRUZ  *Serves 2*

*True American red snapper is one of the most beloved and versatile fish in the sea. It's very white, tender, flaky and mild, yet still holds up to grilling, pan searing or broiling without any problem. Day in and day out, it's hard to go wrong with red snapper. Be sure to look for the true American red snapper, however, as there are many different snappers out there and they are not all created equal in quality; nor do all have the same level of sustainability.*

*I love this sweet, rich and briny kind of sauce when serving dinner to a large party. It can be served family style on a large platter or plated up more formally, portion by portion.*

| | | | | |
|---|---|---|---|---|
| 2 | 6- to 8-ounce snapper fillets | | 5–6 | large green olives, halved or quartered |
| 1/2 | teaspoon Waters Bay Blend (see page 10) | | 3 | tablespoons dry white wine |
| 1 | tablespoon olive oil, divided | | 1 | 14.5-ounce can chopped tomatoes, with juice |
| 1/2 | cup chopped yellow onion | | | Juice of 1 lime |
| 2 | cloves garlic, minced | | 1 | teaspoon agave syrup |
| 1 | jalapeño pepper, seeds and veins optional, minced | | 1 | bay leaf |
| 1 | tablespoon capers, drained | | 1/4 | teaspoon salt |
| | | | 4–5 | sprigs fresh cilantro |

Dust both sides of the snapper fillets with Waters Bay Blend. Heat 1/2 tablespoon olive oil in a large nonstick pan, and sauté the snapper fillets for approximately 2 minutes per side (depending on thickness of the fish). They should be lightly browned on both sides but still raw in the very center. Remove from the pan and place on a warm plate for later.

Using the same pan, add the remaining olive oil and sauté the onion, garlic and jalapeño just until the onion begins to soften. Add the capers and olives and continue sautéing for 1–2 minutes. Deglaze the pan with white wine and reduce by about half. Then add the canned tomatoes, lime juice, agave and bay leaf and bring to a simmer. Simmer for 3–4 minutes, add the sautéed fish to the pan and simmer until the fish is cooked. This should take about 2–3 minutes at most.

Remove the fish from the pan with a large slotted spatula and place on dinner plates. Add salt and reduce the sauce for 1 minute on high heat. Roughly tear the cilantro leaves by hand and add to the pan, or garnish with them at the very end. Just before serving, discard the bay leaf and pour the sauce completely over the fish fillets.

# PAN-SEARED SNOOK WITH SCOTCH BONNETS AND CHERRY TOMATOES   *Serves 2*

*For those of us who like to fly-fish the saltwater flats for bonefish, permit and tarpon (all three of which are generally catch-and-release-only fish), the snook is the one that might end up on the dinner table at the end of a long fishing day. Snook often lie in ambush back in the mangroves, giving fly fishermen a slight chance at a great dinner if they can pinpoint the perfect cast far back into the tree roots. Many anglers heading back to their fishing camp will stop to peruse a few mangroves to see if a willing snook might be lurking in an accessible hide. Also called the robalo, the snook is one of the lightest pure-white-fleshed fish in the ocean, found in the tropical regions of the world. Spicy Scotch bonnet peppers are the perfect complement for this ultra-mild delicacy.*

| | |
|---|---|
| 2 | fillets of snook (roughly 6 ounces each) |
| ½ | teaspoon Waters Bay Blend (see page 10) |
| 1 | teaspoon all-purpose flour |
| ½ | tablespoon canola oil |
| 1 | Scotch bonnet pepper (or habanero) |
| 8–10 | cherry tomatoes, whole |

| | |
|---|---|
| 1 | shallot, finely diced |
| 2 | cloves garlic, minced |
| ½ | cup dry white wine |
| 1 | tablespoon butter |
| | Juice of 1 lime |
| | Pinch of sea salt |
| | Pinch of freshly ground black pepper |
| 6–8 | sprigs fresh cilantro |

Dust both sides of the snook fillets with Waters Bay Blend and coat lightly in flour, shaking off any excess. In a large nonstick pan, sauté the fillets in canola oil for approximately 3 minutes per side, until the fish is lightly browned on both sides and cooked through. Cooking time may vary depending on the thickness of your fish. (If the fish is very thick, it may be necessary to finish cooking it in the oven for a few minutes to get it cooked through without burning the outside.) Once the snook is cooked, remove the fillets to a warm plate while you make the sauce.

Carefully clean the Scotch bonnet pepper, as it can be very hot. (I recommend using gloves.) Remove the stem, seeds and veins of the pepper, then chop the flesh very finely. In the same pan used to cook the fish, add a touch more oil, and then sear the tomatoes until they begin to blister and burst. Lower the heat and add the pepper, shallot and garlic. Sauté until the shallot just begins to soften, then deglaze with white wine. Reduce for 1 full minute, then add in butter and lime juice and swirl the pan constantly until it becomes well incorporated. Season with salt and pepper. Add roughly torn cilantro leaves just before serving. Pour the sauce over the snook and serve.

# SEARED MAHI WITH ARTICHOKES AND CAPERS  *Serves 2*

*Using fresh artichokes for this recipe will certainly create the finest final dish, but canned baby artichokes can be substituted and will cut the preparation time and effort by more than half. Mahi is a fish caught so abundantly around the world that it is usually available in most fish markets all year long. The flesh is somewhat firm and the flavor reasonably mild, which makes it an extremely versatile fish for the chef. Some wines may react strangely on the palate to artichokes, but I've found Riesling and Pinot Blanc to work well with this dish.*

6   fresh baby artichokes or 1 (14-ounce) can baby artichokes, quartered

    Juice of 1 lemon, divided

2   6- to 8-ounce fillets of mahi, boneless and skinless

1/2   teaspoon Waters Bay Blend

1   teaspoon canola oil

1   clove garlic, minced

1   tablespoon capers, drained

1/2   cup dry white wine

1   tablespoon butter

1/2   teaspoon chopped fresh tarragon

1/2   teaspoon chopped fresh oregano

    Pinch of sea salt

    Pinch of freshly ground black pepper

To clean the baby artichokes, snap off the rough, dark green outer leaves by hand until you reach the tender yellow leaves. Cut off the top of the artichokes about 1/2 inch from the tips of the leaves in a straight line across the leaves. Cut off the stem as well. Slice the artichokes into halves or quarters then place immediately in a small bowl of cold water with half of the lemon juice. This will help keep the artichokes from turning brown as you clean each one. Once finished, steam or boil the artichokes for 15 minutes, or until tender, then remove and reserve for later.

Season the mahi fillets well on both sides with Waters Bay Blend. Heat a large nonstick ovenproof pan, then add in the oil and roll it around quickly to coat the bottom. Add the mahi and sear it on high heat. Brown the first side well, (approximately 2 minutes) before turning over. If the fillets are somewhat thin, they can be finished in the pan, but if they are too thick, finish cooking them in a 375-degree oven until done in the center. When the fillets reach an internal temperature of 140 degrees, tested with a meat thermometer, remove the pan from the oven and transfer the fillets to warm plates while the sauce is being prepared.

In the same pan in which the mahi was cooked, quickly sauté the artichokes, garlic and capers for about 1 minute on high. Deglaze the pan with white wine and add the remaining lemon juice. Reduce until the pan is almost dry, and then turn the heat down to low and add the butter and herbs. Swirl the pan constantly until the butter is incorporated, then season with salt and pepper. Pour sauce over the mahi fillets and serve.

# ALMOND-CRUSTED SPECKLED TROUT WITH BROWN BUTTER  *Serves 2*

*This is my favorite take on a classic trout amandine. Speckled trout are the most popular sportfish for those fishing the bays of the Texas Coast. They are very highly regulated and not available for commercial sale in Texas, but I've occasionally found them in some markets in Louisiana and Mississippi. Of course I prefer to catch the specks myself on a fly rod, if I have my choice. Summertime is generally the best season to fish for specks, but they are around all year long. The flesh is mild and flaky, yet strong enough to hold up to many different types of cooking preparations.*

2   6- to 8-ounce fillets of speckled trout

¹/₂   teaspoon sea salt

¹/₄   teaspoon freshly ground black pepper

¹/₂   cup all-purpose flour

2   tablespoons butter, divided

1   tablespoon olive oil

¹/₄   cup sliced almonds, roughly chopped

Juice of 1 lemon

1   teaspoon chopped fresh parsley

Season the trout fillets lightly with sea salt and pepper on both sides and pat dry with paper towels. Dust lightly in flour to coat, shaking off any excess. Add ¹/₂ tablespoon butter and olive oil to a large nonstick pan and gently heat together just until the butter begins to froth and bubble. Lay the trout fillets in the pan carefully and cook over medium heat until they are cooked through, roughly 2 minutes per side; remove to warm dinner plates. Add remaining butter to the pan and cook on high until the butter starts to brown, then add in the almonds and toss to coat. Cook until the almonds are slightly brown, being careful not to let them burn. Add the lemon juice and parsley, and quickly pour the butter over the trout.

# CHILI DUSTED POMPANO     *Serves 2*

*Pompano is one of the finest fish in the Gulf, but it's highly seasonal. When the fish are being caught, it's in large numbers; however, they disappear quickly and are not to be found for long periods of time. When the pompano are running, this simple preparation is one of the easiest and most flavorful ways to enjoy the prized little fish. I love to serve this dish on the skin, as it's very easy to gently remove the flesh from the skin with a fork for each bite. The fillets of pompano have a slightly firm texture and a full, rich flavor that can stand up to earthy spices like ground chili. Typically, pompano are found whole in fish markets, since they usually weigh between 1 and 2 1/2 pounds; most fishmongers will happily fillet them for you. Pompano has a tendency to buckle slightly when cooked on the skin side. To prevent that problem, lightly score the skin by cutting very shallow slices in a crisscross pattern to keep it from buckling when cooking on that side.*

| | |
|---|---|
| 1 whole pompano (roughly a 1 1/2 pound fish) | Sea salt |
| 1/2 teaspoon chili powder | 1 teaspoon vegetable oil |
| Pinch of garlic powder | 1 tablespoon butter |
| Pinch of ground cumin | Juice of 1 lime |

Clean and fillet the pompano if it isn't already filleted, being careful to remove any bones and bloodlines. Combine the chili powder with garlic, cumin and sea salt to taste. Leave the fillets on the skin and season each one heavily on the flesh side. Allow the seasonings to soak in for approximately 10 minutes. Heat a nonstick pan almost to the smoking point, then add in the oil. Place the fillets flesh side down in the hot oil and allow to brown before turning over. Once they have been turned, lightly press down on the fillets with the back side of a fish spatula to keep them from curling up. The fish should be cooked through in about 2 1/2 minutes per side, but check with a thermometer to be sure the internal temperature reaches 140 degrees. Once the fillets are cooked through, remove to dinner plates and allow to rest.

Add butter and lime juice to the hot pan and swirl the pan until the butter emulsifies and incorporates the lime juice completely, then bathe the fish with the warm chili-lime butter.

# SEARED CRAB CAKES WITH SCALLION-LIME AIOLI
*Makes 12–15 cakes*

*Crab cakes are not really a difficult dish to prepare, but they are somewhat expensive. Just as a wine can only be as good as the grapes you grow, crab cakes can only be as good as the crabmeat you start out with. Get the expensive stuff, the fresh jumbo lump crabmeat. Anything with too much breading or filler quickly becomes an ordinary, boring crab-flavored cake, to me. A crab cake should be the celebration of great crabmeat without too many other components to mask its sweet flavor and texture.*

| | |
|---|---|
| 1 pound jumbo lump crabmeat | 1 tablespoon Dijon mustard |
| 1 pound lump crabmeat | 1 tablespoon Worcestershire sauce |
| 1 red bell pepper, finely diced | 1 tablespoon hot sauce |
| 1 bunch scallions, green parts only, chopped | 1 teaspoon Texas Red Dirt Rub, Creole Blend (see page 9) |
| 2 eggs | 1/2 cup panko breadcrumbs |
| 3/4 cup mayonnaise | Butter or vegetable oil for browning |

Pick through the crab for any shell pieces or cartilage. Combine all ingredients, except the crabmeat, in a large mixing bowl and combine well. Gently fold in the crab, being careful not to break apart the big pieces. Form into 2 1/2-ounce cakes (about the size of a large egg) and spread out on a baking sheet. (If the first cake is too wet to hold together, return it to the mixture and add enough panko crumbs just to bind together but don't overdo it.) Finish making the cakes and placing them on the baking sheet. Heat a small amount of butter or oil in a nonstick pan or on a flat griddle, then lightly sear the cakes over medium heat until browned on both sides. Serve hot with Scallion-Lime Aioli.

## SCALLION-LIME AIOLI  *Makes 2 3/4 cups*

| | |
|---|---|
| 2 egg yolks | Juice of 3 limes |
| 2 tablespoons Dijon mustard | 1/4 teaspoon kosher salt |
| 1/2 teaspoon cayenne pepper | 1–2 dashes hot sauce |
| 1 bunch scallions, green parts only, chopped | 2 cups vegetable oil |

In a food processor or blender, combine all ingredients, except for the oil, and blend well. Slowly drizzle in the oil while the machine is running to form a smooth mayonnaise consistency.

# OYSTERS AND SHIITAKES IN BRANDY CREAM SAUCE   *Serves 4*

*For this dish, I often buy the oysters pre-shucked in a jar. I prefer Jeri's brand. This simple dish can turn even those shy about oysters into big fans in a hurry. The herb-laden brandy cream sauce is perfect on a cold evening as an appetizer with a crusty rustic bread. Be sure that the oysters simmer for only a couple of minutes at most. If they overcook, they will become tough and rubbery. If you buy pre-shucked oysters, the entire dish can be prepared in one pan in roughly five minutes, making it one of my all-time favorites!*

| | | | | |
|---|---|---|---|---|
| 1 | tablespoon butter | | 3–4 | sprigs fresh thyme, leaves only, chopped |
| 1 | tablespoon olive oil | | 3 | leaves fresh sage, chopped |
| 1 | small shallot, minced | | 2 | ounces heavy cream |
| 2 | cloves garlic, minced | | | Pinch of sea salt |
| 6–8 | large shiitake mushrooms, stems remove, thinly sliced | | | Pinch of freshly ground black pepper |
| 1 | ounce brandy | | | Bread for dipping |
| 12 | Gulf oysters, freshly shucked | | | |

Combine the butter and olive oil in a hot sauté pan and allow the butter to melt, then add the minced shallots and garlic. Once the shallots begin to soften, add the sliced mushrooms and cook just until they begin to give off some of their juice. Add the brandy while holding the pan off the heat and flame off the alcohol, then reduce until very little liquid remains in the pan. Add all remaining ingredients and simmer on high heat for 1–2 minutes, just until the cream begins to thicken. Serve with warm crusty bread for dipping in the rich sauce.

# NEW ORLEANS–STYLE BARBECUED SHRIMP *Serves 1–2*

*In Texas, we tend to associate the word barbecue with grills and smoke. In this dish, however, it's all done right on the stovetop. This classic New Orleans–style dish is as much about the sauce as it is the shrimp. It can be done with whole, head-on shrimp if you prefer to get some hands dirty, but I tend to use shrimp with only the tail on to make it easier to navigate. Either way, plenty of bread is a must, as the dark, peppery butter sauce is likely to be the most memorable part of the dish.*

| | |
|---|---|
| 8 jumbo wild Gulf shrimp, 10–15 count | 1 teaspoon freshly ground black pepper |
| 12 tablespoons (1 ½ sticks) butter | 1 teaspoon cracked black pepper |
| 1 teaspoon chopped garlic | 1 teaspoon Texas Red Dirt Rub, Creole Blend (see page 9) |
| 4 tablespoons Worcestershire sauce | 1 lemon |
| 3 tablespoons water | Bread |

Remove shells from shrimp, leaving only the tail portion on (optional), then rinse and devein. Cut the butter into 6–8 cubes. In a large nonstick pan, heat the chopped garlic with 1 of the butter cubes just until it begins to bubble, then add all liquids and seasonings. Once the pan comes to a simmer, add the shrimp. Cut the lemon in half and squeeze the juice into the pan, then add the lemon halves as well. Simmer on medium heat until the shrimp are cooked, roughly 2–3 minutes, turning once. Swirl the pan while adding in the remaining butter and continue swirling until the butter has been emulsified into the sauce; then remove the lemon halves and discard. Transfer the shrimp to a large bowl and pour the sauce over the top. Serve with plenty of bread for sopping.

# Seared Tilefish with Tarragon Cream Sauce  *Serves 2*

*Golden tilefish is a bottom-feeding species found predominantly along the Atlantic coastline in relatively deep water. Since tilefish do not migrate, it is easy for a population to quickly become overfished. Numbers that were once in decline are recovering well in the Northern Atlantic, so the sustainability of this fish from the right region is good right now. I love the texture of this fish more than anything else about it. The meat cooks to a snow-white color, with a gorgeous flake that's almost texturally like crabmeat. It is quite seasonal but, when it's available, tilefish is one of my favorite choices for a wide variety of preparations.*

| | | | |
|---|---|---|---|
| 2 | 6- to 8-ounce fillets of golden tilefish, boneless and skinless | 1 | shallot, minced |
| | Sea salt | ½ | cup dry white wine (preferably Sauvignon Blanc) |
| | Freshly ground black pepper | 4 | tablespoons (2 ounces) heavy cream |
| 1 | tablespoon vegetable oil, plus a little more, divided | 3–4 | sprigs fresh tarragon, leaves only, chopped |
| 1 | clove garlic, minced | 2 | teaspoons capers |

Season the fillets well with sea salt and pepper on both sides, then pat dry with paper towels. Heat a large sauté pan until almost smoking, then add 1 tablespoon vegetable oil. Tilt the pan to coat the bottom with a thin layer of oil, then sear the tilefish fillets for 2–3 minutes on each side. The fish should be nicely browned on both sides and just cooked through. If they are too thick to cook through without burning, the fillets can be finished in a 350-degree oven for several minutes. Once the fillets are cooked, remove with a spatula and place on warm dinner plates.

In the same pan in which the fish was cooked, add the garlic and shallots with a touch more oil to sauté. Cook for 20–30 seconds, and then add the white wine. Reduce until the pan is almost dry, then add the cream. Reduce all the way down until the sauce begins to slightly thicken. Add the fresh tarragon and capers. Pour the sauce over the fillets and serve.

# SEARED DOVER SOLE WITH PECAN-BROWN BUTTER AND LUMP CRAB  *Serves 1–2*

*Dover sole is a term often used to label several different species of fish—from sand dabs to gray or lemon sole—but true Dover sole is a completely different quality of fish altogether. Usually, price will be the obvious difference, but always ask your fishmonger if it's really Dover sole before attempting this recipe (only true Dover sole will work in this dish). The simple skeletal structure of this unique fish lends itself well to a whole-fish kind of presentation. The texture of Dover sole is what makes this fish one of the most sought-after in the world, and it's typically going to fetch a high price. It is, however, usually available year-round and freezes well. I love the earthy flavor of brown butter with pecans, and a few sweet bites of crab thrown in make this a rich and decadent dish.*

| | |
|---|---|
| 1 whole Dover sole (about 14–16 ounces) | 3 tablespoons (1 1/2 ounces) butter |
| 1/4 teaspoon Waters Bay Blend (see page 10) | Juice of 1/2 lemon |
| 1 tablespoon vegetable oil | 1/2 teaspoon chopped fresh parsley |
| | 2–3 ounces jumbo lump blue crabmeat |
| | 10–12 pecan halves |

Remove any guts and eggs from the cavity of the Dover sole and rinse well under cold water. Remove the skin from the fish by making a small slit crosswise near the tail and pulling the skin from the flesh, using a kitchen towel for grip if necessary. The skin should be pulled from the fish in one smooth movement. Repeat this on the other side of the fish. Pat the fish dry with paper towels and season with the Waters Bay Blend.

Preheat oven to 375 degrees.

In a hot ovenproof sauté pan, heat the oil and brown the fish well on both sides then place the whole pan into the oven and cook until done, roughly 10 minutes. Once the fish is cooked through, remove from the pan and cut away the head and discard. The top two fillets can be carefully pulled from the body with two spoons. Set aside on another plate. Remove the skeleton and discard. The bones along the back of the fish can also be removed with two spoons and discarded as well, leaving a boneless bottom half fish. Place the top two fillets back on top of the fish to make it look whole, then continue with cooking the sauce.

In the same hot pan in which the fish was cooked, add the butter and cook until it lightly browns. Once lightly browned, add the lemon juice, parsley and crabmeat and simmer for 20–30 seconds. Toss in the pecan halves and stir just until they are coated. Pour the sauce over the Dover sole and serve immediately.

# CRISPY FRIED

Fried fish, in all likelihood, is the most widely craved in the entire realm of fish cooking. Those who aren't that crazy about most fish will still dig in to a crispy fillet, breaded oysters or popcorn shrimp from time to time. A golden brown crunchy outside seems to bring out the best in fish, adding a textural contrast to the delicate flesh and a perfect surface for a great sauce to cling to.

Frying fish is not a technically difficult process, as long as a few simple guidelines are followed. There are basically three types of fried fish: dredged, breaded and battered. The following procedures are a perfect way to get you started in the fish frying game.

## DREDGING:

Dredged fish or shellfish has a light coating on the outside, such as flour or cornmeal. Dredging requires two separate elements to be successful: a liquid (or dunk) and a dry ingredient (or dredge). One of the most common dredging preparations is the combination of buttermilk and flour. To prepare calamari in this style, for example, cut the calamari into rings and soak them in buttermilk. Pull the rings out of the buttermilk and place them into a bowl of flour and toss to coat. The combination of buttermilk and flour work together to form a beautiful crust on the outer surface.

## BREADING:

Breaded fish uses a technique of applying breadcrumbs to the surface of fish before frying. Simply pouring breadcrumbs over fish will not work for frying; the crumbs will fall off. The breading procedure requires three steps. The first is to pat the fish dry with paper towels and then coat it in a light layer of flour. The second step is to dunk the floured fish into a mixture of eggs and milk. The final step is to coat the fish in breadcrumbs. When executed in this order, breading will stick perfectly to the fish and form a golden brown crispy coating when fried.

## BATTERING:

Perhaps the easiest of the frying methods, battered fish is simply a fillet that has been coated in a thick batter and gently dropped into hot oil to fry. A good batter needs to be mixed thoroughly with a whisk to eliminate lumps, and should be just thick enough to coat a fillet completely, but not so thick that the coating becomes thicker than the actual fish once it's cooked. Fillets that are going to be battered need to be dry before dipping in the batter, or the coating will have a hard time sticking to the fish.

# REDFISH CAKES WITH
# SMOKY RÉMOULADE    *Makes 8–10 cakes*

*Fish cakes are a great way to ease people who might be a little squeamish about fish in general into an enjoyment of seafood. Redfish, also called red drum, is a sportfish found wild all along the Gulf Coast from Texas to Florida. However, aquafarms in Texas also produce a tremendous quality of fish. Many aquafarms around the world get a (deservedly) bad reputation for quality and sanitation. The farms in Texas that raise redfish are models of high-quality and environmentally conscious fish farming practices. I use Texas farm-raised redfish on a consistent basis and have never been disappointed. Redfish has a slightly firm but very mild flesh and lends itself to a wide variety of preparations. Snapper, grouper or striped bass can be substituted in this recipe.*

| | |
|---|---|
| 1 | pound redfish fillets, skinless |
| 2 | eggs |
| ¼ | cup mayonnaise |
| | Juice of 1 lime |
| 1 | teaspoon spicy mustard (e.g., Zatarain's) |
| ½ | teaspoon Texas Red Dirt Rub, Creole Blend (see page 9) |
| | Pinch of salt |
| | Pinch of hot smoked paprika |
| ¼ | cup black beans, cooked and drained |

| | |
|---|---|
| 2 | poblano peppers, roasted, peeled and seeded |
| 2 | shallots, finely diced |
| 1 | jalapeño pepper, seeds and veins removed, finely diced |
| | Dash of Worcestershire sauce |
| 1–2 | dashes hot sauce |
| 1 | cup panko breadcrumbs |
| | Vegetable oil for pan-frying or deep-frying |
| | Smoky Rémoulade (see page 111) |

Clean the redfish and dice it into small cubes, being careful to remove any blood lines. Combine with all remaining ingredients—except breadcrumbs, oil and rémoulade—in a mixing bowl and mix well. Form the cakes into 2- to 3-ounce portions, then coat on the outside with the panko crumbs. Pan-fry on both sides or deep-fry until the cakes are crispy and golden brown on the outside and the fish is cooked through. If the cakes are very large, it may be necessary to finish cooking them in a 375-degree oven for a few minutes until done. Serve hot with Smoky Rémoulade spooned over the top or on the side.

## Smoky Rémoulade   *Makes 1 cup*

- 1 tablespoon chipotle puree (canned chipotle in adobo pureed in a blender)
- 2 tablespoons chopped parsley
- 1 tablespoon chopped capers
- 1 teaspoon lemon juice
- 2 teaspoons hot sauce
- 3/4 cup mayonnaise
- 1 teaspoon Texas Red Dirt Rub, Creole Blend (see page 9)
- Salt and freshly ground black pepper to taste

Combine all ingredients and serve with fried redfish cakes.

# FRIED OYSTERS WITH
# JALAPEÑO RÉMOULADE SAUCE *Serves 2–4*

*Raw oysters on the half shell are still my favorite, but it's obviously not a dish for everyone out there. Even the squeamish can be swayed to try oysters when fried properly, though. The key to great fried oysters is to have flavor, such as the hot sauce and seasoning, and to get them crispy in a hurry without overcooking the oysters. I fry oysters at 375 degrees to achieve this balance. Oysters are over 90 percent water, so if they cook very long, the end product becomes shrunken and chewy. A good fried oyster should be plump, crisp and bursting with flavorful juices on the inside, still tasting of the briny ocean just a bit.*

*Fresh oysters are seasonal, of course, and for frying, you cannot beat wild Galveston Bay oysters from the Texas Coast. But many companies sell pasteurized oysters as well. I have found that Jeri's Oyster Company near Galveston sells an outstanding pasteurized oyster in jars, and I've used them many times when the season is tight.*

| | |
|---|---|
| 12 Texas oysters, freshly shucked | 2 cups all-purpose flour |
| 2 tablespoons hot sauce | Vegetable oil for deep-frying |
| 3 tablespoons buttermilk | Jalapeño Rémoulade Sauce |
| 1 tablespoon Texas Red Dirt Rub, Creole Blend (see page 9) | |

Marinate the oysters in a mixture of hot sauce and buttermilk overnight in the fridge. Combine 1 tablespoon of the Creole seasoning mix with the flour, and dredge the oysters in the seasoned flour until well coated. Fry in vegetable oil at 375 degrees until golden brown. This should only take about 1 1/2 minutes. Remove and drain on paper towels. Serve with Jalapeño Rémoulade Sauce.

## JALAPEÑO RÉMOULADE SAUCE *Makes 1 cup*

| | |
|---|---|
| 2 jalapeño peppers | 2 teaspoons hot sauce |
| 2 tablespoons freshly chopped Italian parsley | 3/4 cup mayonnaise |
| 1 tablespoon capers, chopped | Pinch of hot smoked paprika |
| 1 teaspoon lemon juice | 1 teaspoon Texas Red Dirt Rub, Creole Blend (see page 9) |

Roast the jalapeños on the grill or over an open flame (like a gas burner) until charred black on all sides. Once charred, place in a zip lock bag or brown paper bag and allow to sweat for 8–10 minutes. When cool enough to handle, peel and seed the jalapeños then place them in a smoker for 20–25 minutes. Finely dice the smoked jalapeños and combine with the rest of the ingredients in a mixing bowl. Whisk all ingredients together well.

# Crispy Calamari with Citrus-Ginger Dipping Sauce  *Serves 4–6*

*Fried calamari is such a common menu item in restaurants these days that it almost seems silly to put a recipe in this book for it. That being said, not all fried calamari is created equal. The key is to cook the calamari quickly so it becomes tender without getting overcooked and rubbery. Treating calamari the same as fried chicken will do exactly that—turn great calamari into chewy rubber bands. I flash-fry my calamari in oil that's 375 degrees (somewhat hot by most frying standards) so that the coating has a chance to become brown and crisp very quickly. I love this sauce, with its light citrus flavors and bright acidity, to complement the crispy, savory little rings.*

| | |
|---|---|
| 1 pound calamari (tubes only) | 2 cups all-purpose flour |
| 1 cup buttermilk | Vegetable oil for deep-frying |
| 2 tablespoons Texas Red Dirt Rub, Creole Blend (see page 9) | Citrus-Ginger Dipping Sauce |

Rinse the calamari tubes well under cold water and clean them of anything that might be remaining inside. Sometimes a plastic-like quill will be inside, and it needs to be discarded. Cut the tubes into 1/4-inch rings with a sharp knife, then soak the rings in buttermilk for at least 2 hours in the fridge. Combine the Creole Blend with the flour and mix well. Pull the calamari out of the buttermilk and allow most of the excess liquid to drain off, and then place the rings in the seasoned flour mixture. Toss until well coated on all sides. Fry at 375 degrees until crispy, just a minute or so. Remove from the hot oil and place on paper towels to drain. Serve hot with Citrus-Ginger Dipping Sauce.

## Citrus-Ginger Dipping Sauce  *Makes 1 3/4 cups*

| | |
|---|---|
| 1 1/2 cups (12 ounces) ketchup | 3 dashes hot sauce |
| Juice of 1 orange | 1/4 teaspoon freshly grated ginger |
| Juice of 1 lime | Pinch of sea salt |

Combine all ingredients in a mixing bowl and whisk together. Allow to sit for 10–12 minutes before serving.

# GIANT CALAMARI STRIPS *Serves 4*

*Giant calamari comes from a much larger squid than most. It's usually sold in large, thick, flat steaks that have been tenderized to some degree. I typically treat this calamari similar to other types, either cooking it very quickly, or very slowly for a long time. When fried properly, the breadcrumbs that coat the outside are very crispy, while the calamari itself stays tender and juicy. I prefer panko crumbs for this dish for their texture, but other breadcrumbs can work as well.*

2  giant calamari steaks (typically 4–5 ounces each)

1  cup all-purpose flour

1 1/2  cups panko breadcrumbs

1  teaspoon salt, divided

2  eggs

2  ounces whole milk

Vegetable oil for deep-frying

Citrus-Ginger Dipping Sauce (page 115)

Clean the calamari well and cut into 1/2-inch strips. Lay out two shallow pans and fill one with flour, the other with panko crumbs. Season the flour and panko crumbs each with 1/2 teaspoon of salt.

In a mixing bowl, combine the eggs and milk and beat together well, creating an egg wash. Dredge the calamari strips in the seasoned flour, then dip quickly into the egg wash until coated, then into the seasoned panko crumbs. When well coated in the panko, fry in 365-degree oil just until the crumbs are lightly browned on all sides. Drain on paper towels and lightly season with a pinch of salt as soon as they come out of the oil. Serve with Citrus-Ginger Dipping Sauce.

# BEER-BATTERED HALIBUT   *Serves 2–4*

*Anyone who has ever been on a halibut fishing trip in Alaska probably has more fish in the freezer than they know what to do with. Classic fish and chips is one of the most loved and universally acceptable ways to enjoy thick, flaky white fish like halibut; it's one of my go-to meals for groups, especially when kids might be in the mix. The key to a great beer batter is to mix it right at the last second so that the beer doesn't go completely flat before the batter has a chance to cook. Those tiny bubbles left inside give the crust a lighter and better crunch overall. I use wooden skewers to transfer the fish from the batter to the hot oil so that as much of the fish is covered in batter as possible.*

## FOR THE BATTER:

| | |
|---|---|
| 1 cup all-purpose flour | ½ teaspoon sea salt |
| 1 egg yolk | Pinch of cayenne pepper |
| 1 teaspoon sugar | 1 cup Shiner Bock beer |
| ¼ teaspoon baking powder | |

Place all ingredients in a mixing bowl, except for the beer, and whisk together well. Slowly add in the beer while whisking, and stir until a uniform batter is formed.

## FOR THE FISH:

| | |
|---|---|
| 1-pound halibut fillet, boneless and skinless | Vegetable oil for deep-frying |
| 2 teaspoons Waters Bay Blend (see page 10) | Malt vinegar, optional |
| | Jalapeño Rémoulade Sauce (see page 112), optional |

Clean the halibut well and cut into 2- to 4-ounce strips, depending on the thickness of the halibut. Pat the fish dry with paper towels, then season well on all sides with Waters Bay Blend. Dip each piece into the beer batter and coat well on all sides, then drop into 360-degree vegetable oil and fry until golden brown on all sides, turning 2–3 times. Depending on the thickness of the fish, it should fry in approximately 2–3 minutes. Serve with malt vinegar or Jalapeño Rémoulade Sauce.

# CORNMEAL-CRUSTED FLOUNDER WITH SMOKY TOMATO COMPOTE   *Serves 2*

*Flounder is an excellent Gulf sportfish, often caught on rod 'n' reel and sometimes gigged at night under spotlights. The texture is extremely delicate, which is why I often use something like cornmeal to give it a crust and a little more texture. I like to coat just one side of flounder, not adding too much heavy breading but rather just a little texture to the light nature of this delicate fish. The flavor is very sweet, lending itself to many different sauces and seasonings. From other waters, the fluke (pretty much the same fish) can be treated much the same as a nice flounder. I prefer fish that are about 2 pounds or more, since they yield a little thicker fillet.*

| | | | |
|---|---|---|---|
| 4 | tablespoons cornmeal | 2 | 6- to 8-ounce boneless skinless fillets of flounder |
| 1 | teaspoon Waters Bay Blend (see page 10) | 3 | tablespoons vegetable oil |
| | | | Smoky Tomato Compote |

Combine the cornmeal and Waters Bay Blend together and scatter the mixture out on a large dinner plate. Firmly press the flounder fillets down in the cornmeal, coating one side thoroughly. Add the oil to a hot nonstick sauté pan, then place the flounder in gently, cornmeal side down. Cook for 2 minutes on medium heat, until the cornmeal has lightly browned. Turn the fish over and cook until done, likely another minute or 2, depending on the thickness of the flounder. Once cooked, quickly transfer to a plate lined with paper towels and blot off any excess oil before topping with the tomato compote.

## SMOKY TOMATO COMPOTE

| | | | |
|---|---|---|---|
| 4 | large Roma tomatoes | 1 | bay leaf |
| 2 | shallots, minced | | Pinch of cayenne pepper |
| 3 | cloves garlic, minced | 1 | ounce sherry vinegar |
| ¼ | cup extra virgin olive oil | | Pinch of sugar |
| 6 | sprigs fresh thyme | ½ | teaspoon salt |

Begin by blanching all of the tomatoes in boiling water for 25 seconds, then plunging them into ice water. Peel the skins off the tomatoes and place them on a roasting rack. Place the tomatoes in a smoker at 175 degrees for approximately 3–4 minutes, then remove and allow to come to room temperature; chop roughly. The temperature of the smoker is not extremely important, but the tomatoes should absorb some smoke flavor without becoming extremely cooked and mushy.

In a saucepot, lightly sauté the shallots and garlic in olive oil. Once they begin to soften, add the tomatoes and remaining ingredients and cook for 12–15 minutes, or until thick, stirring often. Remove the thyme sprigs and bay leaf and serve.

# CRISPY CATFISH TACOS WITH SPICY SLAW    *Serves 4*

*Fish tacos come in so many shapes and styles that it's hard to know where to start. This particular version is my Texas-style favorite, pairing crispy cornmeal-coated catfish with crispy taco shells and a lightly spicy, zesty slaw to balance out the dish. Catfish is usually very easy to come by in the southern states and is available every day of the year. For a real treat, catch your own channel cat and fry them up fresh. Commercially, wild fresh catfish from Lake Okeechobee is often available and is superior to farm-raised varieties, but frozen catfish fillets from the grocer will work in a pinch.*

| | |
|---|---|
| 3 | large boneless, skinless catfish fillets |
| 1 | cup buttermilk |
| 1 | egg |
| 2 | teaspoons hot sauce |
| 1 1/2 | teaspoons salt (not kosher or coarse salt), divided |
| 2 | cups yellow cornmeal (finely ground cornmeal, not coarse cornmeal) |
| 1 | cup semolina |
| 1 | cup corn flour |

| | |
|---|---|
| 1 | teaspoon ground black pepper |
| 2 | teaspoons Texas Red Dirt Rub, Creole Blend (see page 9) |
| | Vegetable oil (enough to fill your pan 2 inches deep) |
| 10 | yellow corn taco shells |
| | Spicy Slaw (see facing page) |
| | Grated cotija cheese, optional garnish |
| | Fresh cilantro sprigs, optional garnish |
| | Chopped jalapeño, optional garnish |

Cut the catfish fillets into 1–1 1/2 inch-wide strips. Combine the buttermilk, egg, hot sauce and 1/2 teaspoon salt in a mixing bowl and beat together very well. Combine cornmeal, semolina, corn flour, 1 teaspoon salt, pepper, and Creole Blend in another bowl and mix thoroughly, then scatter out onto a large flat dinner plate or baking pan.

Heat a pan of oil to 350 degrees.

Dunk each fillet into the wet mixture until it's coated well on all sides; allow the liquids to drain mostly off, then lay the wet fillets down in the dry mixture. Press each fillet down firmly to be sure the coating is equally applied to all sides of the fish. Pan-fry in 350-degree oil for roughly 4 minutes (depending on the size of your fillets), turning over once. The fish should be floating and lightly browned once it's cooked through. Remove to paper towels to drain. Assemble the tacos, filling each shell with the catfish, Spicy Slaw and your favorite garnishes.

## Spicy Slaw

3 ounces red cabbage, shredded

3 ounces green cabbage, shredded

1 red bell pepper, julienned

2 serrano peppers, finely diced

¼ cup mayonnaise

2 tablespoons sour cream

Pinch of cayenne pepper

¼ teaspoon kosher salt

¼ teaspoon freshly ground black pepper

Juice of 1 lemon

½ teaspoon Texas Red Dirt Rub, Southwestern Blend (see page 9)

Combine all ingredients in a mixing bowl and toss well to incorporate. Allow to marinate at room temperature for at least 45 minutes before serving. Chill are any leftovers.

# PANKO-CRUSTED PAN-FRIED TRIGGERFISH    *Serves 2*

*Triggerfish come in many shapes and sizes, from locations including the colorful coral reefs of the world to the bays and bridge pilings around the Gulf of Mexico. The variety that I've found at fish markets is a diamond-shaped, somewhat gray fish typically found along the Gulf Coast. These oyster and barnacle-eating carnivores have a texture that is unmatched almost anywhere. I've often thought of a fillet of triggerfish as comparable to having a huge slab of crabmeat. As I talked with a large commercial fishing boat crew in Galveston while they unloaded their catch, I noticed three large triggerfish lying in a small bin by themselves. When I inquired as to why, I found out that the three deck hands had hand-picked them as their personal fish to take home to their families. A boat loaded with hundreds of pounds of red snapper, grouper and cobia, yet these guys each picked out a triggerfish. That made quite an impression on me. It's kind of like looking to see what kind of car your mechanic drives.*

| | | | |
|---|---|---|---|
| 1 | pound fresh triggerfish fillets | 2 | ounces milk |
| ¼ | cup all-purpose flour | ½ | cup panko breadcrumbs |
| 1 | teaspoon Waters Bay Blend (see page 10), divided | | Vegetable oil for pan-frying |
| 2 | eggs | | Jalapeño Rémoulade Sauce (see page 112) |

Cut the triggerfish fillets into roughly 4-ounce pieces, but size may vary a little. Rinse and clean them well, then pat dry with paper towels. Set up a breading station to handle the following three steps:

1. Scatter the flour and ¹/₂ teaspoon of Waters Bay Blend on a dinner plate.

2. Mix the eggs with milk and beat together well, then place in a large bowl.

3. Scatter the panko crumbs and ¹/₂ teaspoon of Water Bay Blend on another dinner plate.

Coat each fillet well with the flour mixture, then shake off any excess. Place directly from the flour mix into the egg wash and coat well, then move to the breadcrumbs and coat well. This procedure of flour-egg-breadcrumbs is referred to in professional kitchens as the standard breading procedure. Once the fillets have been breaded, they can be pan-fried. Add vegetable oil to a sauté pan about ¹/₂ inch deep. Heat the oil to roughly 350 degrees. (The easiest test to see if the oil is hot enough is to toss in a pinch of flour or a pinch of breadcrumbs and see if it begins to bubble.) Fry the fillets on each side until they are golden brown and cooked through, roughly 2 minutes per side.

Serve with Jalapeño Rémoulade.

# SHRIMP FRITTERS WITH CAYENNE-LEMON AIOLI  *Serves 4*

*I love a good fritter as an appetizer, a snack, or sometimes even as an entire meal. Be careful not to make these fritters too large, or the shrimp will not cook properly. If shrimp isn't your favorite, crawfish will also work well in this recipe. I first fell in love with fritters made from conch meat, but it's very hard to find these days and not very sustainable, so I tend to avoid conch now.*

| | |
|---|---|
| 8 ounces medium-sized wild-caught Gulf shrimp | ¾ cup all-purpose flour |
| 1 shallot, minced | 1 egg |
| 4 scallions, green parts only, chopped | ½ cup buttermilk |
| 2 cloves garlic, minced | 1 teaspoon Waters Bay Blend (see page 10) |
| ½ poblano pepper, finely diced | ¼ teaspoon baking powder |
| 3 ribs celery, finely diced | Vegetable oil for deep-frying |
| 3–4 good shakes hot sauce | Cayenne-Lemon Aioli |

Peel, clean and devein the shrimp, then cut into small dice. Combine all ingredients in a large mixing bowl and whisk together thoroughly. Drop batter, roughly 1 tablespoon at a time, into 350-degree oil and fry until golden brown, roughly 3 minutes.

## CAYENNE-LEMON AIOLI  *Makes 1¾ cups*

| | |
|---|---|
| 3 egg yolks | 2 dashes hot sauce |
| 1½ teaspoons Dijon mustard | ¼ teaspoon cayenne pepper |
| 1 tablespoon roasted garlic | ½ teaspoon salt |
| Juice of 3 lemons | 1 cup canola oil |
| Zest of 1 lemon | |

Combine all ingredients, except the oil, in a blender or food processor. Puree for 10 seconds, then slowly begin drizzling in the oil a little at a time. Once all of the oil is incorporated, taste and adjust seasonings. A pinch more cayenne can be used to garnish the top of this sauce as well when serving.

# ON THE GRILL

There's something hypnotic about fish cooking on a hot, smoking grill. It's as if instinct draws us to the primitive action of fresh meat being singed by the kiss of raw flames. When food is being cooked outdoors for a party, guests will naturally migrate to the grill and watch without even realizing why. Being able to "man the grill" is an essential skill for anyone hoping to impress guests, especially when the weather turns nice and outdoor parties are in season. (A graceful technique is essential in pulling off a grilled seafood experience and can be the ultimate test of a great host.) While it may seem intimidating, grilling seafood is not as difficult as many believe.

Many types of fish and shellfish are perfect for the grill, but not all fish can handle it. It's important to understand the makeup of different types of fish and whether or not the flesh can stand up to the harsh treatment that a grill can dish out. Fish with slightly firmer flesh or with the skin on are usually suited to this type of cooking. I love fish like mahi, swordfish, cobia, sturgeon, shark and salmon for grilling because they have the right texture and a high enough oil content to absorbs grill flavors well; their flesh is also dense enough not to flake apart while cooking.

While knowing which kinds of fish are suited for grilling is essential to pulling off a great party, proper technique is just as important. The key is to pat the fish dry with paper towels, very lightly coat it with oil and then season it well. If the grill is clean and hot and the fish is dry, lightly coated with oil and seasoned, the odds of success are extremely high.

Grilled fish also needs to be cooked to the right temperature. If it's too rare, some fish is very unappealing, but dry, overcooked fish is just as unpleasant. Firm fish, like those named previously, should be cooked over the highest heat possible to form grill marks on one side and caramelize some of the outer surface.

Once it's time to flip the fish, it should be moved to a cooler section of the grill to finish cooking gently and evenly. Most fish are cooked through when the internal temperature reaches about 140 degrees, so pulling it off the grill around 130–135 degrees is usually ideal as the carryover cooking will finish the job. Knowing how to nail the temperature is half the battle when cooking fish. I recommend an instant-read thermometer to check your fish quickly, but the seasoned grill cook will eventually be able to eyeball when a fillet is cooked through.

*Secret Tip: An extremely easy way to keep fish from sticking to the grill is to cut a potato in half and rub the hot grill bars quickly with the flat side of the raw potato just before you put the fish down. I usually stick a fork in the potato to use as a handle. Strange trick, but it really works!*

# GRILLED MAHI WITH BLACK BEAN, CORN AND CACTUS SALAD  *Serves 2*

*Mahi, also called mahi mahi, dorado or dolphinfish (no, not the Flipper kind of dolphin) is an extremely prolific fish with a huge global range. It's also one of the easiest fish to find fresh all year long. I've heard boat captains refer to these as the chickens of the sea. This is one of my go-to dishes when cooking by the pool in the summer. Having the salad made a few hours before mealtime will make this an easy dish to finish. Simply put on a grilling show and place the fish over the colorful salad and you are all set. And it's quite a healthy meal to boot.*

2   6- to 8-ounce mahi fillets, boneless and skinless

1   teaspoon canola oil

1   teaspoon Waters Bay Blend (see page 10)

    Black Bean, Corn and Cactus Salad (see page 197)

Clean the mahi fillets well, then pat dry with paper towels. Coat each with a thin layer of canola oil on all sides then sprinkle all over with Waters Bay Blend. Cook over high heat on a wood grill until done, approximately 3–4 minutes per side, then remove and serve immediately over a heaping spoonful of Black Bean, Corn and Cactus Salad.

# GRILLED SCALLOP KEBABS ON ROSEMARY SKEWERS WITH HERB BUTTER  *Serves 3–4*

*Scallops are one of my favorite seafood items to grill since they absorb wood smoke flavors beautifully. This dish will only work if the rosemary stems are thick enough to handle the high heat of the grill without catching on fire. While soaking them in water, it might be helpful to place a fork or two on top of the sprigs to keep them weighted down and under water. The singeing rosemary creates a great flavor for the scallops to bask in as they grill.*

| | | | | |
|---|---|---|---|---|
| 3–4 | very large sprigs fresh rosemary | | 2 | sprigs fresh tarragon |
| 12 | large diver scallops (U15 count) | | 2 | sprigs fresh dill |
| | Kosher salt | | 4–6 | leaves fresh basil |
| 2 | tablespoons olive oil | | 4 | ounces (1 stick) butter, softened |
| 2–3 | sprigs fresh thyme | | ½ | teaspoon freshly ground black pepper |

Begin by removing a few of the rosemary leaves from the stems and reserve. Soak the stems in cold water for at least 30 minutes.

Clean the scallops well by removing any small side muscle that may be attached, then pat them dry with a paper towel. Skewer the scallops onto the rosemary stems, leaving a little space between them. Season lightly with about 1 teaspoon salt, then brush a light coating of olive oil on the scallops to keep them from sticking to the grill. Grill over high heat. Watch carefully to make sure the scallops cook and the rosemary doesn't get too burned. Choosing heavy branches of rosemary and soaking them is the key.

Chop the reserved rosemary leaves with all the other fresh herbs. Combine the chopped herbs, softened butter, salt to taste and pepper, and warm gently. Once the scallops have cooked, pull them from the grill and brush heavily with the herbed butter while still hot.

# Wood-Grilled Striped Bass with Baby Shrimp   *Serves 2*

*Wild striped bass swim wild in saltwater and brackish water along the East Coast of the United States. Their meat is somewhat firm and very flavorful, making them popular with chefs all across the country. Hybrid striped bass are similar to the wild species but live in freshwater lakes. Their meat is lighter both in texture and flavor. Several aquafarms also produce hybrid striped bass that I have found to be a high-quality product. The meat from the farmed bass is very flaky and the flavor extremely mild, lending it to many different types of preparation; however, it is very different in overall style to the original wild stripers of the East Coast. Hybrid bass will be more difficult to keep together on the grill, but not impossible. I prefer wild stripers for this dish when I have a choice, but hybrid striper will work, as will red snapper or redfish (red drum). All of these fish readily take on the flavor of wood smoke.*

| | |
|---|---|
| 2 | 6-ounce fillets wild striped bass |
| 1 1/2 | teaspoons Waters Bay Blend (see page 10) |
| 1 | teaspoon vegetable oil |
| 1 | clove garlic, minced |
| 1/2 | tablespoon extra virgin olive oil |
| 1 | ounce dry white wine |
| 3–4 | ounces baby shrimp |
| | Juice of 1/2 lemon |
| 1 | teaspoon chopped fresh basil |
| | Sea salt |
| | Freshly ground black pepper |

Clean and rinse the bass fillets well and pat dry with paper towels. Season with Waters Bay Blend on both sides, then brush with vegetable oil to keep the fish from sticking to the grill. Grill on high heat over pecan wood or mesquite wood until cooked through (150 degrees on a thermometer). This should take about 3–4 minutes per side, depending on your grill and the thickness of the fish. Once cooked, remove to a warm dinner plate.

On a side burner, heat a nonstick pan and sauté the minced garlic in olive oil. Once the garlic has cooked, add the wine and shrimp. Cook until the wine is almost gone, then add the fresh lemon juice and basil. Season with a pinch of salt and pepper, then pour over the grilled striped bass fillets and serve.

Serve over a bed of sautéed julienned vegetables, if desired.

# Grilled Oysters with Garlic and Herbs    *Serves 2–3*

*I had my first grilled oyster in New Orleans several years ago and have been working on my own tech-nique ever since. Oysters really take the flavor of wood smoke well, absorbing the aromatic essence beautifully without getting too smoky. Let 'em sizzle in their own juices with just the right balance of butter and crumb topping and you can make an oyster lover out of almost anybody. Always buy live oysters for this recipe; pasteurized-in-the-shell oysters do not have the right texture for this dish.*

| | |
|---|---|
| 12  fresh live Galveston Bay oysters | 1  teaspoon Texas Red Dirt Rub, Southwestern Blend (see page 9) |
| 8  ounces butter | 1  teaspoon cracked black pepper |
| 2  cloves garlic, minced | Pinch of citric acid |
| ½  teaspoon chopped fresh parsley | Parmesan and Herb Bread-crumbs (see below) |
| ½  teaspoon chopped fresh oregano | |
| Juice and chopped zest of ½ lemon | |

Shuck the oysters and discard the top shells. Set aside.

Combine remaining ingredients in a saucepan and warm through. This sauce must be slightly warm when ladling over grilled oysters or it will solidify.

Place oysters directly over a hot wood-burning grill and allow them to cook in their own half shells for 1–2 minutes, then ladle over the herb-garlic butter. Pour just enough of the butter sauce to fill the oyster shells, letting only small amounts boil over, as too much can cause large flare-ups on the grill. Simmer in this sauce for 1 full minute before removing and placing on a baking sheet.

Top each oyster with a small handful of Parmesan and Herb Breadcrumbs, then place under a broiler just until lightly browned. Keep an eye on them in the broiler. This should only take a min-ute or so.

## Parmesan and herb breadcrumbs

| | |
|---|---|
| ½  cup panko breadcrumbs | 2  tablespoons chopped fresh Italian parsley |
| ½  cup shredded Parmesan cheese | ½  teaspoon salt |

Place all ingredients in a food processor and pulse 5–6 times, until uniformly mixed.

# RED CHILE BARBECUED OYSTERS    *Serves 4–6*

*This sauce works for many different applications, from enchiladas to Mexican casseroles, but I think it works best when paired with the briny, sweet flavor of fresh wild oysters on the grill. The rustic, slightly spicy and earthy notes from the sauce blanket the tender oysters cooked over a wood-burning grill, forming a complex flavor and great texture combination. I love to serve this dish around the pool as guests watch to get the full effect. It pairs really well with a light Pinot Noir or even an earthy Malbec wine.*

| | |
|---|---|
| 24 fresh live Galveston Bay oysters | 1 bunch fresh chives, chopped |
| Guajillo Chile Sauce (see below) | |

Shuck the oysters and discard the top shells. Place the oysters directly over a hot wood-burning grill and allow them to begin cooking in their own half shells for 1–2 minutes. Then ladle over the Guajillo Chile Sauce to fill each shell. Once the oysters begin to bubble in the chile sauce, allow to cook for 1 minute, then remove from the grill and top with freshly chopped chives.

## GUAJILLO CHILE SAUCE    *Makes approximately 4 cups*

| | |
|---|---|
| 1/2 pound dried guajillo chiles, stems and seeds removed | 1 jalapeño pepper, seeds and veins removed |
| 3 cups water | 10 sprigs fresh cilantro |
| 6 Roma tomatoes | 1 small white onion |
| 1/2 poblano pepper, seeds and stem removed | 3 cloves garlic |
| 1 red bell pepper | 1 teaspoon kosher salt |

Place the chiles in a medium-sized saucepot and add the water. Bring to a simmer, cover and allow to simmer on low for 1 1/2–2 hours to soften and rehydrate the chiles. Add remaining ingredients and continue to simmer, partially covered, for 45 minutes. Puree well with a stick blender and strain. Adjust the thickness of the sauce by adding water if it seems too thick, or reducing if it's too thin.

# FIRE-ROASTED JALAPEÑOS WITH SHRIMP   *Serves 4–6*

*Two pieces of equipment will be needed to make this recipe. The first is a jalapeño roasting rack. These come in many shapes and sizes and are very popular at barbecue stores and available on-line as well. If you do a little research, you could probably find one with your favorite sports team's logo etched into it. The second is a jalapeño coring tool. While not absolutely essential, it sure saves time and energy and is fast and efficient for cleaning out the seeds and veins. This dish is somewhat of a "can't miss" around the campfire or at a tailgate. It's as simple as putting the poppers on the grill, pulling down the lid and taking them off when the bacon is done—there's very little room for error and this dish is popular with a crowd.*

4   strips thick bacon

12   fresh jalapeño peppers

5.2-ounce box of Boursin cheese, herb and garlic flavor

12   wild Gulf shrimp, 21–25 count

Parcook the bacon until the fat begins to render; don't let the bacon get crispy. Set aside and let cool.

Pick out the appropriate-size jalapeños to fit in the roasting rack. Once the right-sized jalapeños have been obtained, cut off the stem ends and hollow out the insides, removing the veins and seeds. (Leaving a little bit of the veins will add more heat, as 90 percent of the heat in any pepper is concentrated there; but I prefer to remove as much as possible for this dish.)

Place the cheese in a zip lock bag, microwave for 5 seconds to soften, then cut off just the tip of one corner and use it like a pastry bag. Squeeze a little cheese into each pepper, filling just under the halfway point.

Clean the shrimp and remove the shells (tails optional), then stuff the shrimp inside the pepper as far as it will go. Cut the bacon strips in thirds and top each pepper with a thin piece, securing it in place with a toothpick. The toothpick should go through the bacon, pepper and shrimp and help keep the whole rig together. Place them in the rack and grill over medium heat with the lid pulled down to cook the bacon. Once the bacon is cooked, the poppers are ready. Eat carefully, as the hot cheese can get messy. It's best to let them cool for a few minutes before diving in.

# GRILLED COBIA WITH LEMON BUTTER   *Serves 2*

*Cobia is perhaps my favorite fish in the sea to cook. In Texas they are typically called ling, sometimes lemonfish as well, but whatever name it goes by, this fish always delivers. It's firm enough to be cooked on the grill but also flaky and tender. Cobia has a slight acidic note (probably where the nickname lemonfish came from) and needs very little help to be enjoyed by all fish lovers. When these fish migrate along the beaches from Texas all the way up most of the East Coast, crews from sportfishing vessels and commercial boats alike gaze along the surface looking for these beauties. Most fall in the 15–30 pound range, but 60 pounders and up are also possible. It's typically available from spring through most of the summer, and I recommend this fish over most others as long as it's fresh. I have tried several different types of farm-raised cobia with mixed results, so I still recommend the wild specimens overall. This is a great dish to make when you don't want to get too fancy or do too much work. A simple meal of great grilled fish with a light compound butter is a thing of beauty all by itself.*

| | | | | |
|---|---|---|---|---|
| 2 | 6- to 8-ounce cobia fillets | | 4 | tablespoons unsalted butter, softened |
| ½ | teaspoon Waters Bay Blend (see page 10) | | ¼ | teaspoon granulated garlic |
| | Juice and chopped zest of 1 lemon | | ½ | teaspoon chopped fresh dill |
| | | | 1 | teaspoon vegetable oil |

Season the fish well on all sides with Waters Bay Blend and allow to sit for 10–12 minutes.

Combine the lemon juice and zest, butter, garlic and dill and mix well to form a compound butter. Place the butter mixture on a sheet of plastic wrap and roll into a log shape, then chill well in the refrigerator.

Brush a light coating of oil on the flat sides of the fish before grilling to keep them from sticking to the grill bars. Grill over medium-high heat with the grill cover down until done, roughly 5–6 minutes. Be sure to start with the prettiest side of the fillets (what chefs call the presentation side) facing down. Cook for the first third of the cooking time with the fish at a 45-degree angle to the grill bars. Open the grill cover, pick the fish up and rotate it 90 degrees without flipping; then place it back down on the grill bars. This will form perfect diamond-shaped grill marks on this side of the fish. After two-thirds of the cooking time, turn the fish over and cook the other side. The internal temperature should reach 140 degrees before pulling the fish from the grill. Serve over your favorite side dish with a pat of the lemon butter on top. Be sure to place the butter on the fish while it's still hot so it has a chance to lightly melt and run onto the plate.

# GRILLED WAHOO WITH SWEET POTATO FRIES  *Serves 2*

*Wahoo is one of the fastest-swimming fish in the sea, making it a real challenge for sportsmen. The wahoo's body is long and lean with very firm flesh, almost steak-like. The meat is sweet but also lean so it is extremely important to get the temperature exactly right or the fish can dry out quickly. Use an instant-read thermometer. I love serving a hearty fish like this with the crispy and slightly sweet fries. A light Pinot Noir or rich Chardonnay would pair perfectly with this dish.*

2   6- to 8-ounce wahoo fillets, boneless and skinless

1   teaspoon Waters Bay Blend (see page 10)

1   tablespoon olive oil

Sweet Potato Fries (see page 196)

Clean the wahoo very well and run under cold water. Be sure that any blood lines in the fish are removed. Pat dry with a paper towel, then season well on all sides with Waters Bay Blend. Allow the seasonings to set for 4–5 minutes. Brush the outer surface of the fish lightly with oil, then grill on high over a wood fire until the internal temperature reaches 140 degrees. This should take about 3 minutes per side, depending on how thick your fillets are. Serve with Sweet Potato Fries.

# LIME–MARINATED SWORDFISH STEAKS    *Serves 2*

*Swordfish is a steak-textured fish that holds up exceptionally well on the grill and absorbs other flavors nicely. For years, swordfish numbers were in steady decline and I refused to serve or sell this product. Populations in several areas have rebounded to sufficient levels that I feel more than comfortable featuring it on my menus today. I typically look for day boat swordfish from Hawaii or the Pacific Northwest as the most sustainable, but some North Atlantic fisheries are also doing quite well.*

*It's very important when cleaning your swordfish to remove any traces of the bloodline. Any dark portion of the meat will have a strong flavor and should be trimmed away before cooking.*

| | | | |
|---|---|---|---|
| 2 | 8-ounce swordfish steaks | 1 | teaspoon vegetable oil |
| 1 | tablespoon soy sauce | | Potato Snow (see page 184) |
| | Juice and chopped zest of 2 limes | | Spicy Slaw (see page 123) |

Clean the swordfish well, removing any skin. The meat should be clean and light-colored at this point. Combine the soy sauce, lime juice and zest. Place the swordfish and the marinade in a zip lock bag and remove as much air as possible. Marinate in the refrigerator for 1 hour, turning occasionally so the fish marinates evenly. Remove the fish from the bag and drain off remaining marinade.

Before grilling, brush a light coating of oil on the flat sides of the fish to keep them from sticking. Lay the prettiest side of the fillets (the presentation side) down on the grill at a 45-degree angle to the bars. Grill over medium-high heat with the grill cover down for about 2 minutes. Then lift the cover and pick up the fish and rotate it 90 degrees without flipping over and set back down on the grill bars. This will form perfect diamond-shaped grill marks. Cook with the cover down for 1 $^1/_2$ to 2 minutes more, then turn the fish over and cook until the internal temperature reaches 140 degrees before pulling the fish from the grill. Serve atop Potato Snow and top with Spicy Slaw.

# REDFISH ON THE HALF SHELL    *Serves 2*

*Redfish (or red drum) is one of the great sportfish of the Gulf Coast. This species, once incredibly abundant, had a rapid decline in population during the 1980s as dishes like blackened redfish became popular. Thanks to tighter regulations on sportfishing and commercial harvesting, high-quality aqua-farming practices and the combined efforts of fishermen, fish and game departments, and chefs, the populations of wild redfish are once again strong throughout most of the Gulf. This particular dish is perfect for the angler who just brought home a fish for the grill. Simply fillet the fish, remove any bones and light the fire—not much to it.*

| | | | | |
|---|---|---|---|---|
| 4 | tablespoons butter, softened | | 1/2 | teaspoon Waters Bay Blend (see page 10) |
| 2 | teaspoons chopped shallots | | 2 | fillets boneless redfish, skin on* |
| 1/2 | teaspoon chopped fresh thyme | | 1 | lemon, sliced into thin rounds |
| 1/2 | teaspoon chopped fresh parsley | | | |

Combine the butter, shallots, herbs and Waters Bay Blend and mix thoroughly. Keep at room temperature until ready to use.

Blot the fish dry with paper towels. Brush a light layer of the butter mixture on the skin/scale side of the fish, then turn the fillets over. Brush a somewhat thick layer of the butter mixture on the flesh side and top with several slices of lemon. Cook the fillets skin side down on a grill over low-to-medium heat with the lid closed. The entire cooking process will be done with the skin side down. Depending on the size of the fillets, the cooking time should vary from 12–15 minutes. Once or twice during the cooking process, baste on the remainder of the butter mixture until it's all used. The fish is done when it reaches an internal temperature of 140 degrees.

*I prefer Copper Shoals farm-raised redfish if buying at a store.*

# Spicy Grilled Mako Shark   *Serves 2*

*Shark is a dense, steak-textured fish that holds up well on the grill. Its flavors are somewhat bold as seafood goes, but it's not an overly fishy taste, just bigger flavor than you normally think of for fish. Most species of shark are considered inedible, with a somewhat pronounced ammonia flavor, but a few species—like thresher, blacktip and mako—are actually very good table fare. In many waters, mako shark populations are in such decline that it should not be considered viable for harvest, but the Hawaiian waters have a very healthy and sustainable population right now, so that is my go-to source for mako.*

| | |
|---|---|
| 2  6- to 8-ounce mako shark fillets | ¼  teaspoon freshly ground black pepper |
| ¼  teaspoon sea salt | ½  teaspoon vegetable oil |
| ¼  teaspoon hot smoked paprika | Mashed Potato Cakes (see page 187), optional |
| ¼  teaspoon chile de arbol | Spicy Slaw (see page 123), optional |
| ¼  teaspoon granulated garlic | |

Clean the shark steaks well and remove any skin or red blood lines, then pat dry with paper towels.

Combine all of the seasonings together and rub the shark all over with the blend.

Drizzle the oil over the steaks to apply a thin coating to all sides before grilling. Grill the shark over medium heat on a wood grill, pulling down the lid of your grill to allow as much smoke as possible to penetrate the meat. If using a gas grill, throw a few wood chips over the burners and allow them to catch fire and begin to release smoke before placing the steaks on the grill. Depending on the temperature of the grill and thickness of the steaks, the shark should cook in roughly 2–3 minutes on each side. Use a thermometer to check the internal temperature; it should be 140 degrees. Be very careful not to overcook the shark steaks or they will dry out very quickly. Remove from the grill and serve with Mashed Potato Cakes or Spicy Slaw.

# GRILLED STURGEON    *Serves 2*

*Sturgeon is an incredible fish for the grill, almost meat-like in texture. I sometimes refer to sturgeon as the pork chop of the sea. You can see yellow fat layers marbling the meat of sturgeon, which may seem odd for fish, but don't let that put you off. Although many species of sturgeon are highly protected, and deservedly so, there are sustainable sources of domestic sturgeon in the United States that produce very high-quality fish from the Columbia River.*

| | |
|---|---|
| 2 6- to 8-ounce sturgeon fillets | 1 clove garlic, minced |
| 1 teaspoon Dijon mustard | 1 teaspoon chopped fresh thyme |
| 1 tablespoon dry white wine | 1/2 teaspoon chopped fresh rosemary |
| 1 1/2 teaspoons olive oil | Vegetable oil for the grill |
| 1/2 teaspoon Waters Bay Blend (see page 10) | Herbed Risotto (see page 207) |

Heat a wood-burning grill ahead of time until the wood is burning orange and white coals. Scrub the grill bars well with a wire brush to ensure that they are clean.

Clean and rinse the sturgeon fillets thoroughly with cool water. Combine the mustard, wine, olive oil, Waters Bay Blend, garlic and herbs in a mixing bowl, then use to coat both sides of the sturgeon. Allow to marinate in the refrigerator for at least 30 minutes. Just before grilling the fish, brush the grill bars lightly with a towel soaked in vegetable oil to keep the fish from sticking. Place the sturgeon over the grill on medium heat with the lid closed, and cook until the fish reaches an internal temperature of 145 degrees (approximately 4 minutes on each side). Remove from the grill and serve on top of Herbed Risotto.

# GRILLED OPAH WITH PESTO-INFUSED POLENTA    *Serves 2*

*Opah, also commonly called moonfish, is a fish with a very wide range of ocean in which they are found. Most of the opah that I buy comes from either California or Hawaii, but that isn't the limit to their range by any means. Opah may be one of the strangest looking fish in the sea, but on the plate it is versatile and delicious. The meat is somewhat firm, very similar to tuna, but lighter in color and slightly more delicate. The thick fillet of opah tends to be ideally suited for the grill since its texture allows it to hold up and not fall apart easily; yet when cooked properly, it is fork tender and flakes apart beautifully. Not quite steak-like, but not exactly delicate either, opah is a substantial and firm fish with very mild flavors that's easy to like. Simply grilled, served over flavorful polenta, I love this dish without any additional sauce at all.*

2 6-to 8-ounce Opah fillets

1 teaspoon vegetable oil

1 ½ teaspoon Waters Bay Blend
      (see page 10)

Pesto-Infused Polenta

Sautéed spinach

Season the opah on all sides with Waters Bay Blend and allow to soak in for 10 minutes. Brush a light coating of oil on the flat sides of the fish before grilling to keep them from sticking to the grill bars. Opah can be somewhat thick, so it may be necessary to grill on all sides, rather than just the top and bottom to evenly cook the fish. Grill over medium high heat until done, roughly 5-6 minutes with the grill cover down. Be sure to start with the prettiest side of the fillets (or the presentation side) facing down. Cook for the first third of the cooking time with the fish at a 45 degree angle to the grill bars. Pick the fish up and rotate 90 degrees without flipping over and place back down on the grill bars. This will form perfect diamond shaped grill marks on this side of the fish. Cook the opah on each side evenly to get the center cooked without drying out the outer portion, pulling down the lid of the grill each time. The internal temperature should reach 140 degrees before pulling the fish from the grill, although it's similar to tuna in consistency and can be served somewhat medium rare if you prefer.

Serve with Pesto-Infused Polenta on a bed of sautéed spinach.

# PESTO-INFUSED POLENTA

1 bunch fresh basil, large stems removed

3 cloves garlic, minced, divided

1/4 cup pine nuts, lightly toasted

1 lemon, juice and chopped zest

1/2 cup grated Parmesan cheese, divided

1/4 cup extra virgin olive oil,
   plus 1 tablespoon

1 shallot, minced

1 tablespoon butter

2 1/2 cups chicken stock

1 cup milk

2 cups heavy cream

1 teaspoon salt

1/2 teaspoon cracked black pepper

1 1/2 cups polenta

In a food processor, combine the basil leaves (a few of the smaller stems are fine to leave in), 2 cloves of garlic, pine nuts, lemon juice, zest and half of the Parmesan cheese. Blend while slowly drizzling in the 1/2 cup of extra virgin olive oil. Once the mixture is smooth, reserve the pesto for later.

In a medium saucepot, sauté the shallot and remaining garlic in 1 tablespoon of olive oil and 1 tablespoon of butter just until soft. Add in chicken stock, milk, cream and seasonings and bring to a simmer. Once simmering, whisk in the pesto, followed immediately by the polenta. Simmer very lightly until the polenta begins to thicken. Add in the remaining Parmesan and cook for 10 minutes. Check the consistency at the end. If it seems to thick, adjust with a little more chicken stock. If too thin, reduce slightly.

# CEDAR PLANK WILD SALMON      *Serves 4*

*I love the use of cedar to not only create a visually appealing dish but also to impart an impressive smoky flavor to the salmon. Wild Alaskan salmon is my preference for this dish, but arctic char or trout can also be substituted. I like to cover the top of the salmon with dill, lemon and sea salt while cooking, but typically I'd remove that just before serving to make it easier for the diner. This is a great dish to prepare when guests are coming over and might congregate around the grill. It's a visual show-stopper.*

| | | | | |
|---|---|---|---|---|
| 4 | cedar planks | | 4 | 6-ounce portions wild Alaskan salmon, skin on |
| 2 | tablespoons coarse sea salt | | | |
| 1 | whole bunch fresh dill | | 2 | lemons, sliced into thin rounds |

Soak the cedar planks for at least one hour before beginning this recipe or they will burn too quickly on the grill.

Once soaked, begin by placing a light layer of salt on each plank, roughly the size of the salmon fillet that will go on top. Spread out several sprigs of fresh dill over the salt, then lay the salmon fillets on top, skin side down. Sprinkle additional coarse sea salt evenly over the fish, then lay down more sprigs of fresh dill, finishing the layering with a few slices of lemon on top of each piece of fish. This can be done with larger pieces of salmon, but keep the fish at a size that will stay on the plank without hanging over the edges.

Heat the grill to high, then place the planks directly over high heat and close the lid of the grill. The fish will cook completely on one side without being flipped over, so do not open the lid very many times or the top will have a hard time cooking. Most salmon will take roughly 6–8 minutes to cook, but grills and fish thicknesses vary, so use a thermometer to check for doneness. For medium-rare salmon, remove from the grill at 125 degrees internal temperature; for medium, cook to 135 degrees. While the salmon is cooking, be sure to occasionally check to see that the planks have not caught on fire. Light singeing with black smoking edges is perfect, but have a little water handy in case a large flame ignites. Either pour a little water on the flaming board or use a squirt bottle to shoot down excessive flames. Ideally the salmon should grill, roast and smoke at the same time.

# GRILLED SHRIMP WITH HONEY-BOURBON GLAZE    *Serves 3–4*

*Shrimp on the grill are just about perfect no matter what you add, but the right glaze or sauce can be fantastic. The key to great grilled shrimp begins with picking out the right-size shrimp: they need to be big, so splurge a little. Always find wild domestic shrimp as the foreign farm-raised varieties, although much cheaper, are far inferior in quality and taste and tend to involve horrific environmental practices. Support our American shrimpers whenever you can. I prefer white shrimp, when available, for this dish, but brown shrimp or pink shrimp can work very well too.*

*The other key to grilling shrimp is not to overcook them. Shrimp don't need much time, and they become tough and stringy if you overdo it. Just give 'em enough time to become opaque, brush 'em with plenty of glaze and watch 'em disappear as soon as they hit the plate.*

| | |
|---|---|
| ¼ cup honey | Juice from 1 lemon |
| 1 tablespoon brown sugar | Sea salt and freshly ground black pepper |
| 2 tablespoons Texas bourbon | 10–12 large wild Gulf shrimp |
| 1 tablespoon Dijon mustard | Canola oil |

In a small saucepan, combine honey, sugar, bourbon, mustard, and salt and pepper to taste and simmer for 3–4 minutes, just until slightly thick. Reserve some of the glaze in a dish to use later as a dip. Clean the shrimp well and remove the shells, leaving just the tail portion. Line up shrimp on a cutting board in rows of 3 or 4 and run 2 skewers through each row, leaving just a touch of space between shrimp to allow for even cooking. Season well with salt and pepper and coat lightly with oil before grilling. Lay the shrimp on a hot grill and cook for roughly 2 minutes before turning over, then brush liberally with the glaze repeatedly until cooked through. Serve hot with the reserved glaze as a dipping sauce.

# BACON-WRAPPED SHRIMP BROCHETTE WITH LIME BUTTER    *Serves 3–4*

*Nothing sells to a crowd quite as well as bacon-wrapped shrimp. Of all the parties I've ever catered, I don't know that I've ever had a single bacon-wrapped shrimp left over. It's a marriage of flavors that works for almost every palate. I like the idea of putting a little jalapeño in the middle, but it isn't necessary. Brush on a bit of lime butter and it's just too rich to pass up. Maybe this isn't the most health-conscious dish but, once in a while, I can't resist some succulent indulgence.*

| | | | |
|---|---|---|---|
| 12 | large wild Gulf white shrimp (10-15 count) | 1 | teaspoon Texas Red Dirt Rub, Creole Blend (see page 9) |
| 2 | fresh jalapeño peppers | | Dirty Rice (see page 210) |
| 12 | very thinly sliced strips of bacon | | |

Begin by peeling the shrimp, leaving only the tail shells on. Carefully cut a small slit down the back of each shrimp and remove any vein that may be present.

Slice the jalapeños lengthwise into thin strips, leaving the veins and seeds if you prefer more heat. Place one strip of jalapeño in the slit you've just made in each shrimp, then wrap tightly with a strip of bacon. Use toothpicks (2 may be necessary for really large shrimp) to secure the bacon to the shrimp. After wrapping and stuffing all of the shrimp, season on all sides with the Creole Blend.

Grill over low-to-medium heat until the shrimp are cooked through. For really large shrimp, begin on a grill until the bacon gets somewhat crisp, then finish cooking in an oven, or move to a cooler side of the grill and pull the lid down until finished. Serve over Dirty Rice.

## LIME BUTTER

| | | | |
|---|---|---|---|
| 8 | ounces butter | | Zest from 1 lime |
| ¼ | teaspoon salt | 1 | teaspoon agave nectar |
| | Juice from 2 limes | 6–8 | sprigs fresh cilantro |

In a saucepan, combine all the ingredients, except cilantro, and simmer lightly for 3 minutes. Roughly tear the cilantro leaves by hand and add the last 10–20 seconds. Brush the warm butter generously over the shrimp brochettes after they have cooked.

# ROASTED OR BAKED

One of the most challenging aspects of cooking seafood is keeping the fish from falling apart. Being more tender than most meats, fish is certainly trickier to keep together on the grill and has a higher chance of falling apart in a hot pan. Frying does very well at keeping fish intact, but it can be messy and leaves odor behind when you're done. Sometimes the easiest way to prepare great seafood is simply to turn on the oven. A properly roasted or baked fish dish can be just as satisfying and flavorful as any other type of preparation and typically requires much less skill, finesse, technique and best of all, cleanup. I love the simplicity of just seasoning a fish well, giving it a little flavor enhancement and letting it roast in a hot oven. At times, the easiest method can also be the best.

# CLAMS AND OYSTERS CASINO  *Serves 8–10 as an appetizer*

*This is an easy dish to make for a crowd or dinner party since most of the work can be done a day ahead. The oysters or clams can be stuffed, covered in plastic wrap and set in the fridge overnight. Then they can be pulled straight from the fridge and baked right before serving. When they are bubbling in their shells and lightly golden brown, they are ready to serve.*

| | | | | |
|---|---|---|---|---|
| 2 | jalapeño peppers | | 2 | tablespoons grated Parmesan cheese |
| 1 | Anaheim pepper | | 1 | tablespoon finely chopped parsley |
| 4 | strips bacon | | ¼ | cup panko breadcrumbs |
| 1 | stick (4 ounces) butter | | 2–3 | dashes hot sauce |
| 1 | rib celery, minced | | | Live clams (12 littlenecks or 6 cherrystones) |
| 3 | small cloves garlic, minced | | 12 | live Gulf oysters |
| | Juice of 1 lemon | | | |

Roast the jalapeños and Anaheim pepper until the skins turn black, then allow to sweat in a zip lock bag for 5 minutes. Scrape off the skins and seeds with the back side of a knife, then chop very finely.

Dice the bacon into very small pieces and render until mostly cooked but not quite crispy.

In a large nonstick pan, melt the butter and lightly cook the celery and garlic. Remove from the pan and place in a mixing bowl, then add lemon juice, Parmesan, parsley, breadcrumbs and hot sauce; stir to combine.

Open the clams with a clam knife and discard the top halves of the shells. If using cherrystones, cut each clam into 2 or 3 pieces and then return to the bottom shell. If using littlenecks, leave them whole. Shuck the oysters and discard the top shells.

Preheat oven to 400 degrees.

Top each clam and oyster half with a generous spoonful of the breadcrumb mixture, then bake about 10 minutes, just until the breadcrumbs brown and the clams and oysters are lightly sizzling in their shells. Keep an eye on them to ensure that the crumbs do not burn.

# WHOLE ROASTED POMPANO  *Serves 1–2*

*Pompano are small schooling fish that tend to be all or nothing in terms of availability. When they are running near the beaches, anglers catch them two at a time, but when they retreat to deeper water, they all but disappear. Once in danger from overfishing in Florida, their numbers are quite sustainable these days, so I offer pompano in my restaurants every chance I get. Pompano typically range from 1 to 2½ pounds, making them a perfect choice for roasting whole. Their meat is tender and full-flavored, making them one of the most prized fish in the Gulf for table fare. This dish is simple to make and even easier to like.*

| | | | | |
|---|---|---|---|---|
| 1 | whole pompano, roughly 1½ to 2 pounds | | 2 | teaspoons pink sea salt |
| 1 | tablespoon olive oil | | 6–8 | sprigs fresh dill |
| | | | 1 | lemon, thinly sliced |

The only cleaning required for the pompano is to gut the fish. Rinse well with cold water both inside and outside, allow to dry, then rub all over with olive oil and sea salt (inside the cavity as well).

Preheat oven to 375 degrees.

Place the fish on a sheet pan over a few sprigs of fresh dill, then stuff the inside loosely with lemon slices and remaining dill. Roast for 18–20 minutes, or until done. The internal temperature of the meat should reach 145 degrees. Allow to cool slightly, then serve whole.

# SHRIMP AND CRAWFISH PIE  *Makes 2 large (9 inch) pies*

*Shrimp and crawfish pie is a comfort dish best served in the middle of the table and dished out plate-by-plate after guests are seated. This recipe can be made into small individual pies for single servings, but I prefer the more casual, family-style presentation.*

*Always look for domestic crawfish when buying tail meat; the difference in quality between imported and domestic crawfish is massive. Plenty of Cajun-sounding labels come from China, so be sure to read the labels closely before buying.*

### FOR THE PIE CRUST:

| | |
|---|---|
| 1 1/2 | sticks (6 ounces) butter |
| 4 | tablespoons (2 ounces) lard |
| 2 | cups all-purpose flour |
| 1 | teaspoon iodized salt |
| 1/2 | cup cold water |

Chill all ingredients in the fridge for 1 hour before beginning.

Cut the butter and lard into small chunks. Combine the flour and salt in a mixing bowl, then work in the butter and lard by hand or with a pastry cutter. Mix the dough until it reaches the consistency of wet sand. Add the cold water and mix by hand just until the dough comes together. It's very important not to overmix or overwork this dough so that it doesn't become tough. Roll into a ball and cover with plastic wrap, then refrigerate for at least an hour.

Divide the dough in half and roll to 1/8-inch thickness. Cut out enough dough to line two 9-inch pie pans, and lightly press down the bottoms and the sides to form the bases of the pie shells. There should be enough dough left to cover the top of each pie with a 1/8-inch-thick top layer.

| | | | | |
|---|---|---|---|---|
| 4 | tablespoons (2 ounces) all-purpose flour | | 3 | cloves garlic, minced |
| 1 | stick (4 ounces) butter | | 1 | pound crawfish tails |
| 1 | sweet onion, finely diced | | 1 | pound small Gulf shrimp, peeled and deveined |
| 1 | bunch scallions, chopped | | 2 | tablespoons Texas Red Dirt Rub, Creole Blend (see page 9) |
| 1 | poblano pepper, finely diced, seeds and veins optional | | 4–5 | heavy shakes hot sauce |
| 1 | jalapeño pepper, finely diced, seeds and veins optional | | 1 | cup heavy cream |
| 3 | large ribs celery, diced medium | | 1 | cup chicken stock |
| | | | 1 | cup white wine |

Begin by combining the flour and butter together in a saucepan over medium heat. Cook for a few minutes while stirring to create a roux. The roux should cook for 3–4 minutes, until it begins to lightly turn brown. Add the onion, scallions, peppers, celery and garlic and cook for 2–3 minutes, stirring constantly, just until the vegetables begin to soften. Add remaining ingredients, stir well and simmer for 1 minute. Remove from heat and allow the mix to cool slightly.

Preheat oven to 350 degrees.

Divide the filling between the 2 piecrusts, then cover the tops with another layer of pie crust. Poke a hole in the top of each piecrust to allow steam to release. Bake for 40 minutes, until the piecrust is golden brown on top. Remove from oven and allow to cool for 5–7 minutes before slicing.

# SALMON IN A FOIL POUCH  *Serves 2*

*For anyone who has ever fished for wild salmon, the memory of a stream-side lunch usually tops the list of favorite moments from the trip. There is nothing like the taste and smell of incredibly fresh salmon cooked over an open fire next to the stream where it was caught. This dish is very simple and can be done at home, but in my mind, it's at its best out in the wild. This one is a fisherman's dream.*

| | |
|---|---|
| 1 | 8- to 10-ounce wild Pacific salmon fillet, boneless and skinless |
| ¼ | teaspoon sea salt |
| 5–6 | pink peppercorns, crushed |
| 4–6 | thinly sliced rings white onion |

| | |
|---|---|
| 1 | clove garlic, minced |
| 4–6 | sprigs fresh dill |
| 3–4 | thin lemon slices |
| 1 | teaspoon butter |

Preheat oven to 400 degrees.

Clean the salmon fillet well and be sure to remove any bones. Lay a large sheet of foil down on a countertop, then a second layer directly on top of that. Place the salmon in the center of the double foil layer and season with the salt and pepper. Neatly arrange remaining ingredients on top of the salmon fillet and fold up both layers of foil, sealing the sides well to form a somewhat loose pouch.

Roast in oven until the foil pouch begins to inflate. At that point, remove the pouch from the heat and place on a large dinner plate. Allow salmon to sit and continue steaming inside the sealed pouch for 2–3 minutes before cutting the pouch open. The entire cooking time will usually take about 7–8 minutes, but time can vary substantially, depending on your oven and the size of the salmon. This dish can also be cooked over a grill.

# BRAISED STUFFED CALAMARI   *Serves 6–8*

*Calamari is one of the easiest seafood items to find around the world. It's a very prolific animal and is caught in many places. It also freezes very well so can be stored and transported with ease. There are two basic ways to cook calamari if you want it to be tender. One is to cook it very quickly, such as flash-frying or sautéing on high heat. The other is to cook it for a very long time over low heat. Anything in between turns calamari into the texture of rubber. In this recipe, it's very important to turn the calamari tubes inside out before stuffing them. If you skip this step, the stuffing will not stay inside.*

20 small calamari tubes (bodies only, not the tentacles)

2 1/2 pounds hot Italian sausage, purchased or homemade (see facing page)

2 tablespoons olive oil

2 shallots, minced

2 large ribs celery, finely diced

1 poblano pepper, seeds and veins discarded, finely diced

1 bulb fresh fennel, cored and finely diced (white part only)

3 cloves garlic, minced

6 tablespoons (3 ounces) dry white wine

1 15-ounce can tomato puree or tomato sauce

1 cup chicken stock

1 14 1/2-ounce can diced tomatoes

1/2 teaspoon dried basil

1/2 teaspoon dried oregano

1 teaspoon salt

1/2 teaspoon freshly ground black pepper

Wild Rice Pilaf (see page 213)

Begin by cleaning the calamari tubes and removing anything that might be inside. Turn the tubes inside out with your finger before stuffing them. Stuff each inverted tube with enough sausage to just fill; do not overstuff them or they will burst when cooking. In a large Dutch oven–style pot, heat 1 tablespoon oil and brown the outsides of the stuffed calamari slightly; then remove from the pan and set aside on a plate.

To the same pot, add remaining 1 tablespoon of oil, shallots, celery, pepper, fennel and garlic and sauté until slightly softened. Deglaze the pan with white wine and reduce for 1 minute. Add the remaining ingredients, except pilaf, and stir together well. Place the stuffed calamari back into the mixture and bring to a light simmer. Cover with a tight-fitting lid and simmer on low for 1 hour (or cook in the oven at 225 degrees for 1 hour). Serve over Wild Rice Pilaf with plenty of sauce to accompany.

*\* If the purchased sausage you want to use is not available in bulk, buy it in casing, then remove it from the casing before stuffing into the calamari.*

## Hot Italian Sausage

| | |
|---|---|
| 2 ½ pounds ground pork | 2 tablespoons fresh chopped oregano |
| 1 ½ tablespoons kosher salt | 2 tablespoons fresh chopped basil |
| 1 tablespoon sugar | 1 tablespoon red chile flakes |
| 1 tablespoon fennel seeds | 1 teaspoon freshly ground black pepper |
| 1 ½ teaspoons ground coriander | 6 tablespoons water |
| 1 ½ teaspoons Hungarian paprika | 2 tablespoons red wine vinegar |
| ¼ teaspoon ground cayenne pepper | |

Mix all ingredients in a large mixing bowl and combine well. Allow to sit for at least 10 minutes before using.

# ROASTED STEELHEAD WITH DILL    *Serves 2*

*Steelhead is one of the most challenging sportfish to catch, but it's also one of the most rewarding on the plate. Although genetically the same fish as a rainbow trout, steelhead differentiate themselves from rainbows by migrating rather than living their entire lives in the same body of water. Some journey out to sea and gorge on shrimp; others migrate from large lakes up into rivers to spawn. But all steelhead tend to develop a rich, orange-colored, salmon-like flesh. Several aquaculture facilities have begun to produce steelhead in ocean pens with very good results. My favorite sells under the name Tasmanian Ocean Trout, which has a beautiful light salmon flavor and tender flake. This recipe is simple to execute, celebrating the natural flavor and texture of this prized fish with just a few complementary flavors. This dish pairs well with a citrusy Sauvignon Blanc or a light Pinot Noir.*

| | | | |
|---|---|---|---|
| 1 | lemon | 1 | teaspoon sea salt |
| 2 | 8-ounce fillets steelhead trout, skin on | | Freshly ground black pepper |
| 2 | bunches fresh dill | | Herb-Roasted Fingerling Potatoes (see page 191) |

Preheat oven to 425 degrees.

Zest the lemon, then slice into thin rounds.

Clean the fish well and remove any bones, but leave the skin attached. Blot dry with paper towels. Place a thick layer of the fresh whole dill sprigs in a nonstick pan, then place the fillets skin side down on top of the dill. Top each fillet with the lemon zest and season with salt and a light grinding of pepper. Remove most of the stems from the remaining dill, and place a thin layer of the dill on top of each fillet. Top with lemon rounds. Roast in oven for 6–7 minutes, or until cooked through. The internal temperature should be 130 degrees. Serve over Herb-Roasted Fingerling Potatoes.

# OYSTER PAN ROAST    *Serves 8*

*This rich casserole-type dish is nothing short of pure indulgence. I love to serve this dish in social settings like dinner parties or even for big football games. My favorite presentation method is to bring it bubbling hot to a standing appetizer table and serve with breads or crackers for sopping up all the decadent sauce. My favorite wine pairing for this dish is rich, buttery Chardonnay.*

| | | | |
|---|---|---|---|
| 24 | live oysters | | Pinch of rubbed sage |
| 1 | tablespoon butter | | Pinch of celery salt |
| 1 | tablespoon olive oil | 3–4 | heavy shakes hot sauce |
| 3 | cloves garlic, minced | 6 | tablespoons heavy cream |
| 1 | tablespoon Pernod liqueur | ¼ | cup panko breadcrumbs |
| 2 | tablespoons chopped fresh chives | 3 | tablespoons grated Parmesan cheese |
| ½ | teaspoon chopped fresh thyme | | Crusty bread for dipping |

Shuck the oysters and discard the shells. (If you prefer, the oysters can be purchased pre-shucked in a jar. I like the Jeri's brand.)

Heat a large sauté pan to medium and add the butter, olive oil and garlic. Sauté the garlic lightly but do not let it brown. Deglaze the pan with Pernod. Add the oysters, herbs, celery salt, hot sauce and cream. Simmer lightly until the cream starts to thicken. Remove from heat and top with breadcrumbs and Parmesan. Move pan under a broiler until the tops are nicely browned. Serve with rustic crusty bread for dipping.

# HOT CRAB DIP  *Serves 8–10*

*Crab is one of my favorite ingredients. I use fresh blue crab from the Gulf, typically either jumbo lump or lump. This dip is the perfect kind of dish to bring to a Super Bowl party, baby shower or any informal social gathering. It's very easy to make ahead and pop into the oven right before serving. While pasteurized crabmeat may be an acceptable substitute for fresh, never let me catch you using crab that's spelled with a "K."*

| | |
|---|---|
| 6 tablespoons butter | 2 lemons |
| 2/3 cup panko breadcrumbs | 1 tablespoon Texas Red Dirt Rub, Creole Blend (see page 9) |
| 2 bunches scallions, chopped | 6–8 healthy shakes hot sauce |
| 2 ribs celery, finely diced | 2 shakes Worcestershire sauce |
| 3 cloves garlic, minced | 8 ounces jumbo lump blue crabmeat |
| 2 tablespoons chopped fresh thyme | 8 ounces blue crab claw meat |
| 1 pound soft cream cheese, room temperature | Crackers or bread for serving |
| 2/3 cup mayonnaise | |

Preheat oven to 325 degrees.

Melt the butter and pour over the panko breadcrumbs; toss to combine. Set aside.

In a mixing bowl, combine remaining ingredients, except the crab, and stir well. Once the mixture has a soft and smooth consistency, gently fold in the crab, being careful not to break up the large pieces. Spread into a buttered 2-quart casserole dish or larger and sprinkle the buttered breadcrumbs over the top. Bake for 40 minutes, or until the top is nicely browned and the dip is bubbling. Serve with your favorite crackers, flatbreads or toast points.

# SIDES

Although I've had many stream-side lunches consisting of nothing more than fresh fish, man cannot live on fish alone. Seafood may occupy the center stage, but there still needs to be a little something on the side to complete a truly great meal. In this chapter, I've gathered many of my favorite sides to accompany seafood dishes and even included a few that have seafood in the recipe.

# CUCUMBER SLAW   *Serves 4*

*This lightly flavored slaw works extremely well with cold fish dishes like smoked salmon. I usually leave the peel on the cucumber for added texture and fiber, but remember to wash them before using.*

| | |
|---|---|
| 2 English cucumbers | ½ teaspoon celery salt |
| 2 Roma tomatoes | ¼ teaspoon freshly ground black pepper |
| 4–6 sprigs fresh dill, chopped | Juice and chopped zest of 1 lemon |
| 3 tablespoons chopped fresh chives | 3 tablespoons mayonnaise |

Cut the cucumbers in half lengthwise and remove any seeds in the middle by raking a spoon across them. Cut into long julienne strips; I prefer using a mandolin to cut them, as it makes a more uniform cut than a knife, but this isn't necessary. Cut the Roma tomatoes in half and remove most of the seeds, then cut into julienne strips. Combine all ingredients together and serve chilled.


# JICAMA AND CITRUS SLAW   *Serves 3–4*

*Jicama is one of my favorite ingredients for adding texture and crunch—but not a distinctive or over-whelming flavor—to a fresh salad or slaw. This slaw already has plenty going on with the pickled jalapeños and citrus notes, while the jicama lends plenty of vitamins and dietary fiber to this healthy side dish.*

| | |
|---|---|
| 1 whole jicama, peeled and julienned | 2 oranges |
| 2 fresh jalapeño peppers, julienned | 1 tablespoon extra virgin olive oil |
| ½ purple onion, julienned | Juice of ½ lemon |
| Juice of 3 limes | ½ teaspoon salt |
| Pinch of salt | Pinch of freshly ground black pepper |

In a mixing bowl, combine the julienned jicama, jalapeños and onion with the lime juice and a pinch of salt. Allow them to pickle together for at least 2 hours, then drain off the excess lime juice.

Supreme the oranges (remove individual sections from membrane) and reserve any extra juice. Add the oranges to the bowl along with remaining ingredients, and toss together.

# SHAVED FENNEL SLAW     *Serves 4*

*Fresh fennel is a bulb somewhat resembling celery, with dill-like fronds on the top. The flavor has a very mild anise-licorice note that lends well to pairing with many light seafood varieties. When cooked it is very aromatic, but raw it's crunchy and light, which makes it a favorite for me in the heat of summer. This slaw can be made without the serrano pepper if the heat level is more than your crowd can handle, but I like a little spicy heat in this dish, especially in the summer. I suggest having a mandolin handy for this recipe, it will save you a tremendous amount of time.*

| | | | |
|---|---|---|---|
| 1 | fresh fennel bulb | | Juice of 1 lime |
| 5 | ounces radish (3–4 radishes) | 2–4 | tablespoons mayonnaise |
| 1 | serrano pepper | ¼ | teaspoon salt |
| 4 | ounces hearts of palm (about half a jar) | 2 | pinches freshly ground black pepper |

Remove the hard core of the fennel bulb, then use a mandolin or a very sharp knife to shave the fennel as thinly as possible. Place in a mixing bowl.

Wash the radishes under cold water and scrub to remove any dirt, but do not peel. With the mandolin or knife, julienne the radishes into very long, thin strips and shave the serrano very thin. Add to the fennel.

Cut the hearts of palm into half moons and add to the bowl. Chop a few fennel fronds and add to the other ingredients. Add lime juice, mayonnaise, and seasonings. Mix together and taste; adjust salt and pepper if desired.

# POTATO SNOW  *Serves 3–4*

*I love to serve this version of potato snow just as it comes out of the ricer. The texture is very fun, and the cream and butter really give some great flavor without being completely unhealthy, since most of it gets left behind in the pot. For the utmost in richness, of course it can be ladled right on top of the snow, but I typically use little, if any.*

2 1/2   pounds Yukon gold potatoes

5   cloves garlic, minced

2   cups heavy cream

2   cups milk

4   ounces (1 stick) butter

2   teaspoons kosher salt

1/2   teaspoon freshly ground black pepper

Peel the potatoes and cut into large chunks. Combine all of the other ingredients into a saucepot and bring to a simmer. Add the potatoes and simmer until they become very soft, typically about 40 minutes, depending on the size of your chunks. Remove a few chunks at a time with a slotted spoon and place into a hand-held potato-ricer. Squeeze the potato out of the ricer, creating the "snow" texture as it falls onto the plate. This can be served as is, or a tiny drizzle of the cooking cream can be added for extra richness.

# MASHED POTATO CAKES   *Serves 8*

*For this recipe, you must start with mashed potatoes that have been cooked and chilled completely in the refrigerator. As much as I love mashed potatoes, I think I actually prefer them on the second day—pan-fried and with a nice, crunchy surface.*

| | | | |
|---|---|---|---|
| 1 | pound (2 cups) day-old mashed potatoes | 4 | tablespoons milk |
| | All-purpose flour | | Panko breadcrumbs |
| 2 | eggs | | Vegetable oil |

Form the mashed potatoes into puck-shaped cakes, roughly 2 ounces each. To bread the cakes, coat in flour, dip in egg wash (eggs and milk beaten together), and coat entire outer surface with panko breadcrumbs. (See page 108 for more about breading.)

Once all of the cakes are breaded, heat 1 inch of vegetable oil in a skillet to 350 degrees. Add the cakes to the skillet and lightly brown on both sides. Remove cakes with a slotted spatula and drain on paper towels.

## ROASTED GARLIC MASHED POTATOES   *Serves 6–8*

*This is my go-to recipe for mashed potatoes—a real family and crowd pleaser.*

| | | | |
|---|---|---|---|
| 1 | head of garlic | 2 | teaspoons kosher salt |
| 1 | cup heavy cream | | Pinch of freshly ground black pepper |
| 1/2 | cup sour cream | 3 | pounds russet potatoes (peeling optional) |
| 4 | tablespoons unsalted butter | | |

In a 325-degree oven, roast the garlic until it becomes soft and golden brown, roughly 45 minutes. Allow to cool just until you can handle it, then cut the pod in half and squeeze out all of the roasted garlic into a pan, leaving the papery skins behind. Combine the garlic with the cream, sour cream, butter and seasonings and heat gently.

Cut the potatoes into rough chunks and boil until soft, about 40 minutes, depending on the size of your chunks. Drain the potatoes, then pour the creamy mixture over the top and mash together while they are still hot.

# RED POTATOES WITH PECAN PESTO    *Serves 6–8*

*Potatoes are so commonly served that I constantly try to find new ways to vary them. This dish is anything but boring, bringing a bright acidity and light herb flavor with a nutty texture to simple potatoes. This pesto also makes a great pasta sauce with a little cream added to thin it out slightly.*

| | | |
|---|---|---|
| 8 | quarts water | 10–15 red bliss potatoes, scrubbed and quartered |
| 2 | tablespoons kosher salt | Pecan Pesto (see below) |

In a large pot, bring water to a boil and add kosher salt. Add potatoes and let simmer for 30–35 minutes, until you can pierce them with a fork. Strain and cool. Just before serving, quickly roast the potatoes in a 450-degree oven for just a few minutes. Remove potatoes to a plate and drizzle the Pecan Pesto on top. Sprinkle with a few pecans to finish.

## PECAN PESTO    *Makes 2 1/3 cups*

| | | | |
|---|---|---|---|
| 1 | bunch fresh basil, most stems removed | | Juice of 1 lemon |
| 1 | bunch cilantro, most stems removed | 1/2 | teaspoon kosher salt |
| 1/2 | cup grated Parmesan cheese | 1/2 | cup toasted pecans, divided |
| | | 1 | cup extra virgin olive oil |

Add all ingredients to a food processor, except for the oil and half of the pecans. Chop until the ingredients are well blended, then slowly drizzle in the oil while the machine is running. Use remaining pecans for garnish.

# WARM GERMAN-STYLE POTATO SALAD *Serves 6–8*

*This German-inspired potato salad pairs nicely with many different dishes, but I love it with fish because of its richness from the bacon, bright flavors of dill and intense acidity. It's important to pour the dressing over the potatoes while they are still warm to ensure that the flavors are absorbed. The salad can be refrigerated and warmed again the next day, but it will have a much better texture if served fresh.*

Plenty of salt

2 pounds fingerling potatoes (I like multiple colors)

2 ounces bacon, diced

1 small purple onion, finely diced

1/2 cup apple cider vinegar

1/2 cup whole grain mustard

1/4 cup sour cream

1/2 bunch fresh dill, chopped

1 bunch green onions, green parts only, chopped

Fill a pot halfway with water and bring to a boil. Add small handfuls of salt until it tastes almost as salty as the ocean. Boil the whole potatoes in salted water until soft, and then drain well and place in a large mixing bowl.

In a sauté pan, slowly render the bacon over medium heat until almost crisp, then add the diced onion and cook until just softened. Add the vinegar and mustard, whisk all together and then remove from the heat. Allow to cool for 10 minutes, then add the sour cream, dill and green onions. Pour over the warm potatoes and toss well to coat. Serve warm.

# HERB-ROASTED FINGERLING POTATOES   *Serves 8–10*

*Fingerling potatoes come in an array of shapes, sizes and colors and make a great side for many fish dishes. This recipe is fairly simple to pull off and will work for most types of small potatoes. If you want to substitute larger potatoes, cut them down in size and they can be roasted in the same fashion. This dish will be best right out of the oven, when the potatoes are still sizzling and golden brown on the outside.*

| | | | |
|---|---|---|---|
| 3 | pounds fingerling potatoes | 2 | teaspoons kosher salt |
| 1 | red bell pepper, medium dice | 1/4 | teaspoon freshly ground black pepper |
| 1 | poblano pepper, medium dice | 4 | tablespoons olive oil |
| 1 | Texas 1015 sweet onion, large dice | 1 | tablespoon Worcestershire sauce |
| 2 | teaspoons dried basil | | Juice of 1 lemon |
| 1 | teaspoon dried thyme | | |

Preheat oven to 400 degrees.

Cut the fingerlings into halves. Toss well in a large mixing bowl with remaining ingredients. Pour the contents into a large roasting pan and roast in oven until the potatoes are soft and golden brown on the outside. This should take approximately 40 minutes in a convection oven, but the time may vary, depending on the size of the potato pieces and type of oven. While the potatoes are cooking, open the oven and stir the mixture every 15 minutes to prevent sticking.

POTATO GAUFRETTES

# POTATO GAUFRETTES    *Serves 6*

*This simple yet fancy-looking potato chip is a perfect side item for almost any dish. I prefer this style to most chips because it has more surface area to come in contact with the hot oil, which results in crispier potato chips. To be extra fancy, try drizzling a touch of white winter truffle oil on them right before serving, or sprinkle with truffle salt.*

|   |   |   |
|---|---|---|
| 2 | large potatoes | Salt |
|   | Oil for deep-frying |   |

Peel the potatoes and slice with a mandolin. On the mandolin, use the waffle shaped blade, turning the potato $^1/_4$ rotation after each slice. The first chip will not turn out right, but each one after that should. The thickness should be adjusted so that each slice has little holes showing through in the crisscross pattern. Right after slicing, drop the chips into cold water until ready to fry.

Deep-fry in 365-degree vegetable oil until lightly golden brown and crisp. Quickly drain on paper towels and sprinkle with salt.

# SWEET POTATO CHIPS    *Serves 6*

*Sweet potatoes come in orange and purple colors. Both work well for frying into chips, but they should be fried separately since they can vary in cooking times.*

|   |   |   |
|---|---|---|
| 2 | large sweet potatoes | Salt |
|   | Oil for deep-frying |   |

Peel the sweet potatoes with a vegetable peeler and slice very thinly. I prefer to use a mandolin for uniformity. Soak the slices in cold water for 15–20 minutes to remove some of the starch.

Heat oil for deep-frying in a deep, heavy pot to 275 degrees. Drain the potato slices well, then fry in batches until the chips are no longer bubbling. Since the oil is somewhat lower in temperature for frying, this may take 10–15 minutes per batch. Once they have stopped bubbling, drain on paper towels and sprinkle immediately with salt, while still hot. The chips will need to rest for at least 6–8 minutes to ensure a crispy texture. If they come out chewy rather than crisp, they were cut too thick, not fried long enough or didn't rest long enough after cooking.

# SWEET POTATO GRITS  *Serves 10–12*

*I've become quite famous for my different versions of grits, and this recipe is one of my all-time favorites. The sweet potatoes balance the savory ingredients to create a dish that pairs well with many different entrées, especially seafood. I strongly recommend using stone-ground grits, but instant will work in a pinch.*

| | |
|---|---|
| 1–2 | sweet potatoes (to make 3 cups puree) |
| 2 | tablespoons canola oil |
| 1 | small white onion, diced |
| 4 | cloves garlic, minced |
| 1½ | quarts chicken stock |
| 2 | cups heavy cream |

| | |
|---|---|
| 1 | teaspoon salt |
| 1 | teaspoon chili powder |
| | Pinch of cayenne pepper |
| 2 | cups grated cheddar cheese |
| 1 | pound stone-ground grits |
| 1 | teaspoon salt |

Peel sweet potatoes, cut into large pieces, and boil until soft. Drain, then puree in a food processor until smooth; reserve.

Heat the oil in a large saucepot, and sweat the onion and garlic until the onion begins to soften. Add the chicken stock and cream to the pot and bring to a simmer. Next add the seasonings and cheese, then whisk briskly while slowly adding the grits. Bring the mixture back to a light simmer and cook for 18–20 minutes (5 minutes, if using instant grits), until the grits have cooked. Be sure to stir every couple of minutes to keep the grits from sticking to the bottom of the pan. Once cooked, fold in the sweet potato puree and serve hot.

# SWEET POTATO FRIES   *Serves 6–8*

*A Japanese mandolin, also called a Japanese turning vegetable slicer, is required to make this dish properly. They typically run about forty bucks but can be used for many different and interesting presentations. This piece of equipment is tremendously easy and fast to operate. It has a crank handle on one end and fine cutting plates on the other, so using one is as easy as setting the blades, inserting a sweet potato and giving the handle a turn.*

*These crispy little fried sweet potato nests are a great addition to grilled fish. I love their crunchy texture and salty yet slightly sweet flavor.*

| | |
|---|---|
| 2   orange sweet potatoes | Sea salt |
| Oil for deep-frying | |

Peel the sweet potatoes with a vegetable peeler. Using a Japanese mandolin, turn the sweet potatoes with the crank handle to form small corkscrew-shaped threads. Once they have been turned on the machine, soak them in cold water for at least 10 minutes to help remove some of their starch. Pull the "nests" out of the cold water and allow to drain well, then shake off any remaining water.

Heat oil to 325-degrees. Using tongs, add individual nests of potatoes to the oil and fry until they turn golden brown and the oil completely stops bubbling. Turn the nests over in the oil once or twice while frying to ensure even cooking. Once done, drain the potatoes on paper towels and sprinkle liberally with sea salt.

# BLACK BEAN, CORN AND CACTUS SALAD   *Serves 6*

*Loaded with vitamins and flavor, this dish complements grilled fish or chicken and is a very healthy alternative to typical high-carb sides like pasta or potato salad. It makes a flavorful accompaniment for many different proteins and really works well in the summer when you need something substantial but don't want to fill up too much during the day.*

2   tablespoons extra virgin olive oil, plus more for drizzling, divided

2   ears fresh corn

3   paddles fresh cactus (also called nopales)

1   teaspoon Texas Red Dirt Rub, Creole Blend (see page 9)

1   clove garlic, minced

    Juice of 2 lemons

5–6   sprigs fresh cilantro, chopped

½   teaspoon salt

1   15-ounce can black beans, drained

2   ribs celery, diced

Lightly drizzle oil over the corn and cactus paddles on all sides, then season with Creole Blend. Place on high heat over a wood grill. Turn the corn every minute or so until many of the kernels begin to turn lightly golden brown, then remove from the grill. The cactus paddles should be flipped after 2 minutes, and then cooked until they begin to bubble from the inside. Remove from the grill and allow to cool slightly.

Place the garlic, lemon juice, cilantro and salt in a large mixing bowl and stir. Allow to sit for at least 5 minutes.

Dice the cactus into large cubes, and remove the corn from the cob with a chef's knife.

Add the corn, cactus, beans, celery and 2 tablespoons olive oil to the bowl. Mix well and serve.

# SPICY SWEET CORN CAKES   *Serves 8–10*

*Corn cakes are as simple to cook as pancakes, but are more complex in seasoning and flavor. As an accompaniment to many seafood items, they act not only as a flavor component but also as a vessel for savoring that last bit of sauce. Using a nonstick griddle is easiest for these cakes, but nonstick spray or a touch of butter added to your favorite pan or cast iron works equally well.*

| | | | | |
|---|---|---|---|---|
| 3 | ears fresh corn | | | Pinch of ground cumin |
| 2 | jalapeño peppers | | | Pinch of coriander |
| 1 | cup coarse yellow cornmeal (stone-ground if possible) | | 2 | tablespoons melted butter |
| 1/2 | cup all-purpose flour | | 1/2 | cup buttermilk |
| 3/4 | teaspoon baking powder | | 1/2 | cup heavy cream |
| 1/2 | teaspoon granulated garlic | | 2 | eggs |
| 1 | teaspoon sugar | | 1 1/2 | teaspoons honey |
| 1 | teaspoon salt | | 1 | cup grated white cheddar cheese |
| 1/4 | teaspoon cayenne pepper | | 1 | shallot, minced |

Grill the corn—in the husks—and jalapeños together over high heat. Remove the jalapeños when they have blackened on all sides, then allow them to sweat in a zip lock bag or paper sack for 5–10 minutes. Let the corn cook until the outsides have all turned black, then pull from the grill and allow to steam in the husks for 10 minutes.

Scrape off the black outer skin from the jalapeños with the back of a knife. Remove the seeds and veins, or leave the seeds and veins in if you like more heat. Cut the jalapeños into fine dice. Place in a medium-sized bowl.

Remove the husks from the corn and cut the corn off the cobs with a sharp knife. Add corn to the jalapeños.

Combine the cornmeal, flour, baking powder, garlic and spices in a mixing bowl and whisk together until well incorporated.

Combine the butter, buttermilk, cream, eggs and honey in another bowl and whisk well. Add the wet ingredients to the dry ingredients and stir, then fold in the cheese, jalapeños, corn and shallot.

Heat a griddle on medium heat and treat with nonstick spray if you wish. Scoop out the batter in 1/4-cup portions and spread on hot griddle in the same fashion as for making pancakes. Cook the corn cakes over medium heat for 2–3 minutes per side, until golden brown on both sides, then serve hot.

# ANDOUILLE HUSHPUPPIES   *Serves 6–8*

*Hushpuppies are a natural accompaniment to fish, especially fried fish. In this version, I like to take hushpuppies to a higher level with the addition of smoky Andouille sausage. It was my wife who first suggested adding something meaty to a standard hushpuppy, and I've been making it this way ever since. It really makes the fried treats more complex and interesting. I like to serve these with a side of Smoky Rémoulade sauce.*

|        | Oil for deep-frying |
| ------ | ---- |
| 1 ½ | cups cornmeal |
| ½ | cup all-purpose flour |
| 1 | teaspoon baking powder |
| 2 | teaspoons Texas Red Dirt Rub, Creole Blend (see page 9) |
| 1 | teaspoon kosher salt |
| ¼ | yellow onion, finely diced (about ½ cup) |
| 1 | poblano pepper, roasted, peeled, seeded and diced |
| 1 | tablespoon hot sauce |
| 2 | eggs |
| 1 | cup buttermilk |
| 4 | ounces smoked Andouille sausage, finely diced |
|   | Smoky Rémoulade sauce (see page 111) |

Heat oil to 350 degrees in a deep, heavy pot.

Combine remaining ingredients in a mixing bowl and whisk together thoroughly.

Scoop out a heavy spoonful of batter and carefully drop into hot oil using a second spoon to scrape from the first one. Add more spoonfuls of batter but do not let the oil temperature drop much below 350. Deep-fry in small batches until golden brown on all sides, rolling them over from time to time to ensure even cooking. Drain on paper towels and serve hot.

# CRAWPUPPIES   *Serves 6–8*

*Hushpuppies typically work well when served with fish, but this version is pretty substantial on its own. I like to serve these as party appetizers, especially for informal parties like sporting events.*

1 1/2   cups cornmeal

1/2   cup all-purpose flour

1   teaspoon baking powder

2   teaspoons Texas Red Dirt Rub, Creole Blend (see page 9)

1   teaspoon kosher salt

1/4   teaspoon Hungarian paprika

1   bunch scallions, white and green parts, chopped

2   jalapeño peppers, finely diced

1 1/2   tablespoons hot sauce

2   eggs

1   cup buttermilk

2   ounces smoked Andouille sausage, finely diced

8   ounces crawfish tail meat

   Oil for frying

Combine all ingredients, except the oil, in a mixing bowl and whisk together thoroughly.

Heat oil to 350 degrees in a deep, heavy pot.

Scoop out a heavy spoonful of batter and carefully drop into hot oil using a second spoon to scrape from the first one. Deep-fry in small batches until golden brown on all sides, rolling them over from time to time to ensure even cooking. Drain on paper towels and serve hot.

# BACON-LACED BRUSSELS SPROUTS   *Serves 4–6*

*If you think you hate Brussels sprouts, try them one more time—with bacon. When done properly, lightly browned on the outside with just a hint of smoky bacon surrounding them, Brussels sprouts are a real crowd pleaser. I sometimes pull the leaves apart and lightly sauté them rather than cutting into quarters; this can help anyone who has an issue with the texture of this vegetable—even the little guys. Either way, Brussels sprouts are a great pairing for fish and this dish can help boost their poor reputation.*

| | | | | |
|---|---|---|---|---|
| 1 | pound Brussels sprouts | | 1 | clove garlic, chopped |
| | Juice of 1 lemon | | 1 | tablespoon Dijon mustard |
| 4 | ounces bacon, diced | | 3 | tablespoons sherry vinegar |
| 1 | tablespoon extra virgin olive oil | | 1 | teaspoon salt |
| ½ | purple onion, thinly julienned | | ½ | teaspoon freshly ground black pepper |

Trim the Brussels sprouts and cut into quarters. In a medium-sized soup pot, simmer enough salted water to cover the Brussels sprouts (heavy salting, almost like the sea). Add the lemon juice, then blanch the Brussels sprouts for approximately 5–7 minutes, until slightly tender. The time may vary depending on the size of your sprouts. Drain and shock the sprouts in an ice bath to stop the cooking. After the sprouts have cooled, drain and set aside.

In a large sauté pan, render the bacon until almost crisp. Add a drizzle of olive oil along with the onion and garlic and cook until soft. Add the sprouts to the pan, turn up the heat and sauté very quickly until lightly browned. Then add the mustard and vinegar and season with salt and pepper. Reduce the resulting sauce slightly, toss to coat and serve hot.

# GREEN BEAN CASSEROLE   *Serves 8–10*

*I've had plenty of green bean casseroles that begin with a can of cream of this or that, but I just cannot, in good conscience, cook from a can for my family. Here's a crowd-pleasing comfort dish loaded with enough flavor to make even picky kids get excited about green beans.*

| | |
|---|---|
| 1 | pound fresh green beans, ends trimmed |
| 4 | ounces bacon, diced |
| 1 | large yellow onion, chopped |
| 4 | cloves garlic, minced |
| 1 | tablespoon olive oil |
| 1½ | tablespoons butter |

| | |
|---|---|
| 12 | ounces button mushrooms, sliced |
| 2 | tablespoons all-purpose flour |
| 1 | cup chicken stock |
| 1 | cup heavy cream |
| 2 | ounces Parmesan cheese |
| 1 | teaspoon kosher salt |
| | Crispy Fried Shallots (see below) |

Boil the green beans in heavily salted water (salty like the ocean) for 6 minutes, then plunge into ice water to stop the cooking. Drain and place into a medium-size casserole dish. In a large saucepot, render the bacon until almost crispy then add the onion, garlic, olive oil and butter. Sweat for 2 minutes, then add mushrooms and cook until they have lost their liquid. Add flour and cook for 1 full minute. Add the stock and cream and simmer until just slightly thick, then add the cheese and salt.

Preheat oven to 350 degrees.

Pour the sauce over the green beans and stir to combine. Bake for 10–15 minutes, until bubbling hot. Top with crispy fried shallots.

## CRISPY FRIED SHALLOTS

| | |
|---|---|
| 5 | shallots |
| 2 | cups buttermilk |
| 1 | tablespoon hot sauce |

| | |
|---|---|
| 2 | tablespoons Texas Red Dirt Rub, Creole Blend (see page 9) |
| 2 | cups all-purpose flour |

Peel the shallots and cut into rings. Soak them for at least 10 minutes in a mixture of buttermilk and hot sauce. Add the seasoning to the flour and mix. Pull the shallots from the buttermilk, draining as much off as possible, and coat them in the flour mixture. Fry in 350-degree oil until golden brown and crispy. Drain on paper towels.

# SOUTHERN SUCCOTASH   *Serves 6–8*

*Succotash is typically a celebration of spring and early summer in the South, showcasing the best of what the farmers have to offer. The ingredients can certainly vary, depending on what is in season, but a mixture of peas, fresh beans, corn and aromatic vegetables, quickly sautéed and seasoned properly, is the general idea.*

| | |
|---|---|
| 1   tablespoon canola oil | 1   ear fresh corn, shucked and cut from the cob |
| 1   tablespoon butter | 1   cup fresh English peas |
| 1   small yellow onion, finely diced | ½   cup cooked lima beans |
| 1   carrot, finely diced | 1   tablespoon Texas Red Dirt Rub, Creole Blend (see page 9) |
| 2   ribs celery, finely diced | |
| 1   red bell pepper, finely diced | |

Heat the oil and butter over medium-high heat in a large pan. Add the onion, carrot, celery and pepper and sauté over medium-to-high heat for 2 minutes. Add the remaining ingredients and continue to sauté for an additional 5 minutes. Serve hot.

# FRIED SPINACH   *Serves 3–4*

*For anyone who believes there is nothing to like about spinach, try it fried and you might change your mind. Be careful when you add the spinach to the oil. The oil will spatter and pop for a little while as the water cooks out of the spinach leaves. Of course, it's not quite as healthy as a fresh spinach salad, but fried spinach is very easy to love.*

| | |
|---|---|
| 1   pound fresh baby spinach | Salt |
| Oil for deep-frying | |

Wash the spinach and dry it well to reduce the amount of spattering.

Heat oil to 365 degrees in a deep, heavy pot. Once dry, toss the spinach into the hot oil. Move the leaves around in the oil, turning over once or twice while they fry. Once the oil becomes still (quits bubbling), remove the spinach and drain on paper towels. Sprinkle with plenty of salt.

# Lobster Mac and Cheese   *Serves 8*

*This dish is good old-fashioned comfort food, but all grown up and made decadent. Mac and cheese brings back fond memories for almost everyone I know, and adding lobster to anything makes it irresistible. The key here is to use fresh lobster and not overcook it. When it's done properly, this dish is truly a can't-miss home run effort. It is expensive, but when it's time to impress, this is a no-brainer.*

| | |
|---|---|
| 2 | small lobsters (1 pounders) or 1 large lobster (2 ½ pounder) |
| 1 | tablespoon butter |
| 1 | tablespoon all-purpose flour |
| 1 ½ | cups half-and-half |
| | Sea salt |
| | Ground white pepper |

| | |
|---|---|
| 2 | ounces grated Chihuahua cheese |
| 1 | 5.2-ounce box Boursin Garlic and Fine Herbs cheese |
| 4 | cups cooked macaroni elbows |
| 2 | sprigs fresh tarragon, leaves chopped |
| 3–4 | sprigs fresh dill, fronds chopped |
| 1 | Roma tomato, seeded and diced |

Steam or boil the lobsters (the seafood counter will usually do this for you if you like) until done, then chill. Remove the meat from the tails, legs and claws and cut into large chunks. Set aside.

In a large saucepot, add the butter and flour and cook, stirring until a light roux has formed. Do not brown, but rather cook just until the flour is bubbling and begins to smell like sourdough toast. Add the half-and-half and bring to a simmer while whisking. Season to taste with salt and white pepper. Once the mixture has simmered for 2 minutes, add the cheeses and cook until melted. Then add the lobster meat, macaroni, herbs and diced tomato. Fold together until all ingredients are incorporated and serve immediately.

# HERBED RISOTTO    *Serves 8–10*

*Risotto is a dish that requires a lot of stirring and labor. When done correctly the dish should be creamy and rich, full of fresh herb flavor. I'm sorry to say that I know of no acceptable shortcut to making great risotto but when it's good, it's really good and well worth the effort.*

| | |
|---|---|
| 1 quart chicken stock | 1/2 cup dry white wine |
| 1 1/2 teaspoons kosher salt | 1 tablespoon chopped fresh Italian parsley |
| 2 shallots, diced | 1 tablespoon chopped fresh basil |
| 3 cloves garlic, minced | 2 teaspoons chopped fresh rosemary |
| 1 tablespoon olive oil | 2 teaspoons chopped fresh thyme |
| 3 tablespoons butter, divided | 1/4 cup grated Parmesan cheese |
| 1 1/2 cups Arborio rice | |

Heat the chicken stock and salt in a saucepan and hold. In a large heavy-bottomed saucepot, sweat the shallot and garlic in oil and 1 tablespoon of butter until soft. Then add the rice. Cook together for 2 minutes while stirring, being careful not to let the rice turn brown. Add the wine and stir constantly until completely absorbed. Add a ladle of hot chicken stock and repeat the last step, stirring until the liquid is absorbed. Repeat until only a couple ladlesful of stock remain. Stir in the herbs, remaining butter and cheese. Now add the remaining stock a ladleful at a time, as before. Once all of the stock is absorbed, the risotto should be done.

# WILD MUSHROOMS AND BARLEY   *Serves 4–6*

*Barley is a tasty starch option, especially when combined with the savory richness of wild mushrooms. When serving with fish, I let any juices or sauce drip down and become part of the overall barley mixture. This dish complements heavy, steak-like fish such as sturgeon, opah or swordfish. The flavors pair nicely with earthy Pinot Noir or Chianti.*

| | |
|---|---|
| 1 ½   cups quick-cooking barley | Chicken stock |

Cook the barley in chicken stock according to package directions, as different brands of barley vary drastically in cooking times.

| | | | |
|---|---|---|---|
| 2 | tablespoons olive oil | ¼ | cup dry white wine |
| 1 | shallot, finely diced | ½ | teaspoon chopped fresh thyme |
| 2 | cloves garlic, minced | ½ | teaspoon salt |
| 1 | cup roughly chopped crimini mushrooms | ¼ | teaspoon freshly ground black pepper |
| 1 | cup sliced shiitake mushrooms | | |

Heat the oil in a heavy-bottomed saucepot and sweat the shallots and garlic until soft. Add the mushrooms and cook until they have lost some of their juices. Deglaze the pot with white wine, then add the remaining ingredients, including the cooked barley. Cook until the pan is almost dry, then serve.

# DIRTY RICE   *Serves 6–8*

*Most authentic dirty rice contains livers of some sort. I tend to shy away from organ meats, so this version is somewhat tamer but still packed with intensity. I like rice in general, but on its own, it seems somewhat bland. Add all of these ingredients and rice becomes a completely different dish altogether—the dirtier the better.*

½  pound tasso, finely diced

½  pound Andouille bulk sausage (not in casing)

1  small sweet onion, diced

2  ribs celery, diced

1  poblano pepper, diced

3  cloves garlic, minced

2  cups cooked plain white rice

Texas Red Dirt Rub, Creole Blend (see page 9)

In a large sauté pan, render the tasso on low heat until it releases much of its fat, then add the sausage and continue cooking. Once the sausage is cooked, add the onion, celery, poblano and garlic; cover and cook until very soft. Stir in the cooked rice and add a pinch of Texas Red Dirt Rub, Creole Blend, if desired.

# WILD RICE PILAF  *Serves 6–8*

*Wild rice isn't technically in the rice family at all; it's more of a wild grass grain. Its flavors are very nutty and earthy, yet they tend to need a little help from other savory flavors to make a complete dish. I like to use jasmine rice along with wild rice, although they have different cooking times; so pay careful attention to how long each step takes to ensure that each rice gets cooked properly.*

| | | | | |
|---|---|---|---|---|
| 1 | small sweet onion, finely diced | | 1 | teaspoon chopped fresh thyme |
| 3 | cloves garlic, minced | | 1 | tablespoon chopped fresh parsley |
| 2 | tablespoons butter | | 1 | teaspoon kosher salt |
| 1/2 | cup uncooked wild rice | | 1/4 | teaspoon freshly ground black pepper |
| 3 1/2 | cups chicken stock | | 1 | bunch scallions, green parts only, chopped |
| 1 | cup uncooked white jasmine rice | | | |

In a large saucepan, sweat the onions and garlic in butter until soft, then add the wild rice. Sauté together for 1 full minute while stirring. Add the chicken stock and bring to a simmer; cover with a lid and simmer for 25 minutes. Add remaining ingredients, except green onions, and simmer covered for an additional 20 minutes. Fluff with a fork when cooked, then add chopped green onions just before serving.

# Southwestern Orzo Pasta Salad   *Serves 6*

*This pasta salad is bursting with bright flavors, making it a match for almost any light seafood dish from shrimp to trout. Orzo absorbs other flavors well and is easy to eat without too much mess. Be sure to cook orzo, and other pastas for that matter, in heavily salted water, almost as salty as the ocean.*

1  cup Waters Restaurant House Dressing (see page 37)

2  cups orzo pasta, cooked (makes 4 cups)

3  Roma tomatoes, diced

1  small purple onion, julienned

½  cup shredded Parmesan cheese

   Pinch of kosher salt

   Pinch of freshly ground black pepper

6–8  sprigs fresh cilantro

Combine all ingredients, except cilantro, together and mix well. Allow the salad to sit in the refrigerator for at least 1 hour before serving. Garnish with a little fresh cilantro.

# INDEX

# Metric Conversion Chart

| VOLUME MEASUREMENTS | | WEIGHT MEASUREMENTS | | TEMPERATURE CONVERSION | |
|---|---|---|---|---|---|
| U.S. | Metric | U.S. | Metric | Fahrenheit | Celsius |
| 1 teaspoon | 5 ml | $^1/_2$ ounce | 15 g | 250 | 120 |
| 1 tablespoon | 15 ml | 1 ounce | 30 g | 300 | 150 |
| $^1/_4$ cup | 60 ml | 3 ounces | 90 g | 325 | 160 |
| $^1/_3$ cup | 75 ml | 4 ounces | 115 g | 350 | 180 |
| $^1/_2$ cup | 125 ml | 8 ounces | 225 g | 375 | 190 |
| $^2/_3$ cup | 150 ml | 12 ounces | 350 g | 400 | 200 |
| $^3/_4$ cup | 175 ml | 1 pound | 450 g | 425 | 220 |
| 1 cup | 250 ml | $2^1/_4$ pounds | 1 kg | 450 | 230 |